Guide to
FSU
&
TALLAHASSEE

❖

Murray D. Laurie

PINEAPPLE PRESS, INC.
Sarasota, Florida

Inquiries should be addressed to:

Pineapple Press, Inc.
P.O. Box 3899
Sarasota, Florida 34230
www.pineapplepress.com.

Library of Congress Cataloging in Publication Data

Laurie, Murray D., 1934-
    Guide to FSU and Tallahassee / Murray D. Laurie. — 1st ed.
        p.   cm.
    Includes bibliographical references (p.   ) and index.
    ISBN 1-56164-184-7 (pb : alk. paper)
    1. Florida State University. 2. Florida State University Pictorial works. 3. Tallahassee (Fla.)—Description and travel. I. Title.
    LD1771.F93L38   1999
    378.759'88-dc21
                                                    99-23103
                                                    CIP

First Edition
10 9 8 7 6 5 4 3 2 1

Design by *Osprey Design Systems*
Printed and bound by Versa Press, East Peoria, Illinois

Photographs by Murray D. Laurie
Maps by William Martino

Dedication

To my father, John F. Durack, who sent all five of his children off to Tallahassee to earn their degrees at FSU and never regretted it for a moment.

Table of Contents

Introduction

As the site of a large pre-Columbian settlement and an important sixteenth-century Spanish mission, and of the state's capital since the 1820s, Tallahassee has seen its share of history. The center of government for one of the nation's fastest-growing states, it is a vibrant and expanding metropolis, yet one that has made an effort to hold onto its heritage, its historic buildings, and its tradition of Southern hospitality. Through words and pictures this book will introduce visitors and residents alike to some of the city's most interesting features, old and new. A brief historical sketch links many of the included sites with events in the city's development.

Tallahassee first captured my heart over forty years ago when I was a student at Florida State University. Exploring the Tallahassee of today is still a rich and enlightening experience. There are surprises in out-of-the-way corners as well as cherished can't-miss-it landmarks. Much of the old city has retained its graceful manner, and treasures that were there all along, like the Knott House, the Riley House, the Old City Cemetery, Maclay Gardens, and Goodwood, look better than ever.

Also looking better than ever is the campus of Florida State University, from the welcoming view of the gates, the fountain, and Westcott at the crest of College Avenue to the dazzling splendor of the new University Center embracing Doak Campbell Stadium on the west side of the campus.

I relished my freshman year at FSU: living in what seemed like an ancient castle, learning to serve tea with elegance and style in the lounge at Bryan Hall, getting red clay all over my new tennis shoes when it rained, feeling the muscles in my legs ache from climbing hills I wasn't used to, running back to the lecture hall with wet hair after a swimming class in Montgomery Gym, dangling from a trapeze on the circus lot, walking over to the stadium on a crisp fall afternoon with a crowd of friends to cheer for the Garnet and Gold.

It's not often that you get a chance to recapture happy times and bring your early impressions up to date. I am grateful to June Cussen at Pineapple Press for letting me follow this dream, to introduce others not only to the city of Tallahassee but also to the main buildings and sites on the Florida State University campus.

The brief historical sketch of FSU aspires to outline and shade in some of the people and events that have contributed to the growth of the university. I've tried to convey a sense of the history and function of each building included in this book and to provide some background on the person for whom the building was named. Because I am intrigued by each building's appearance and visual distinctions, I couldn't resist offering a few architectural details. Photographing each structure helped me focus not only on its unique features but on the extraordinary diversity and character of the campus as a whole.

I've had the good fortune to spend the last twenty years documenting Florida's historic buildings and writing about its history, architecture, and museums. It is my hope that this book will give pleasure to those who know Tallahassee and Florida State University well and introduce newcomers to the city and the campus in a friendly and interesting fashion.

I am indebted to kind individuals at the Tallahassee Historic Preservation Foundation, the Bureau of Historic Preservation, Tours with a Southern Accent, the Special Collections Room of the Strozier Library, the FSU Facilities Planning office, and many other departments on campus for their help with my research. This refresher course in Tallahassee and Florida State University was made all the more enjoyable by the kindness of friends and fellow Seminoles such as Sudye Cauthen, Ruth Blitch, Stephen Edwards, Beverly Spencer, and Betty Lou Joanos.

As the first in my family to attend FSU, I set the course for my sisters and my brother. Ardent gratitude is extended to my parents,

John and Emily Durack, who proudly sent all five of us to Florida State University: Margaret Durack Stuckemeyer (FSU '60), Michael O'Rourke Durack (FSU '66), Maureen Durack Mulrooney (FSU '68), and Joan Durack Jenkins (FSU '69).

Murray Durack Laurie (FSU '56)

1

Tallahassee

A Historical Sketch
of Tallahassee

Tallahassee, which, according to most sources, means "old town" or "old fields," attracted settlers long before it was chosen as the capital of Florida in the nineteenth century. The Lake Jackson mound builders found this a pleasant place to live almost eleven thousand years ago—and why not? The seven gentle hills offered splendid vistas and an abundance of natural home sites. The soil was rich and the climate mild. Freshwater lakes provided food and water for drinking and irrigating fields. As their name suggests, these early settlers constructed high earthen mounds, atop which temples were placed to pay homage to the magnanimous gods.

When the proud Spanish soldiers led by Hernando de Soto marched through the area with their clanking armor and fearsome horses and dogs in the sixteenth century, they noted the region's advantages for future exploration and exploitation. After establishing a foothold on the peninsula at St. Augustine and Pensacola in the 1600s, the Spanish made contact with the Apalachee Indians living in the "old town." They sent priests and soldiers and settlers to bring their European ways to this rich interior, founding a series of missions—like links in a chain. Luckily, we can catch glimmers of these distant events today by visiting the Lake Jackson site and Mission San Luis de Apalachee, where archaeologists gently brush away the dust of time to reveal the past.

But raids by British and Creek Indian forces destroyed the mission chain and once more the "old fields" were abandoned, only to be rediscovered by Seminole Indians moving south from Georgia and Alabama. White settlers also moved into this wilderness and claimed this good land, setting up a clash of cultures once more as Florida became a territory of the United States of America in 1821. To unite East and West Florida, with their capitals at St. Augustine and Pensacola, respectively, leaders of the new territory chose Tallahassee, a point about halfway between the two, as the new capital. The first quarter section of land was laid out, surrounded by a cleared area measuring two hundred feet. Within this section today are many government office buildings, the central business district, and Park Avenue, originally known as Two Hundred Foot Street.

Although the first legislative body met in a log cabin, this was soon replaced by a two-story building with slender pillars and verandas. Wealthy cotton planters and businessmen staked claims in the new capital and built handsome neoclassical mansions such as The Columns and Goodwood. Soon churches with lofty spires such as the First Presbyterian Church lifted the tone of the community. To create added glamour, a full township was offered to the Marquis de Lafayette to persuade him to come to Florida. Although he never came, another well-connected Frenchman, Achille Murat, nephew of Napoleon Bonaparte, did make Tallahassee his home. He married a lovely widow named Catherine Willis, the great-grandniece of George Washington. The royal pair is buried in Tallahassee. Catherine Murat's delightful *petite maison*, Bellevue, is one of the best reasons to visit the Tallahassee Museum of History and Natural Science, where it stands among an ensemble of other historic buildings.

To link the inland city to the coast, Florida's first railroad, operated as a mule-drawn affair, was built from Tallahassee to St. Marks on the Gulf. The rail bed is still used as a recreation corridor, and passengers still board the train at the old railroad station, built in the 1850s.

When Florida became a state in 1845, a brand-new capitol building stood ready. It forms the core of the Old Capitol, which now closely resembles the 1902 version with additional wings and an imposing dome. A visit to the restored building, a museum of

Florida's political past, is an enlightening experience. The same may be said for a stop at the Union Bank building across Monroe Street. Constructed in the 1840s, it is now a museum devoted to the history of the African American contribution to the state.

Led by Mayor Francis Eppes in 1854, the city constructed a seminary building on Gallows Hill west of the center of town, thus transforming a gruesome site of final justice into a setting devoted to education and progress. It is now the home of Florida State University. Florida left the Union to join the Confederacy in 1861, and its capital was the only one in the South not captured by Federal forces, although they came close. A band made up partly of young cadets from the West Florida Seminary (FSU's forerunner) held off the soldiers at the Battle of Natural Bridge. However, Union soldiers did arrive in Tallahassee after the Civil War was over, occupying some of the elegant homes on Park Avenue, such as the Knott House, for a time during Reconstruction.

Visitors to Tallahassee in the 1870s described it as an "old city" with a pleasing and comfortable atmosphere, neat cottages and handsome mansions, an abundance of flowers, and a refined and cultured society. We see evidence of this gracious city today in the Park Avenue and Calhoun Street Historic Districts with their beautifully restored homes and graceful gardens. This Tallahassee was a far cry from the rip-roaring, rowdy frontier hamlet, its muddy streets filled with wandering livestock, that had been reported less than fifty years earlier.

By the turn of the century, two institutions of higher learning added luster to the capital city—Florida State College, later to become FSU, and Florida State Normal and Industrial School, now FAMU. A library named for its founder David Walker was chartered; its comely building is still standing on Park Avenue, close to downtown Tallahassee. Wooden stores and commercial buildings were replaced by brick buildings with fancy Victorian touches such as the grillwork on the balconies for Gallie's Hall, and the gingerbread dressing up the facades of the new hotels that catered to the state's movers and shakers, particularly when the legislature was in session. Stroll along Adams or Monroe Street near the capitol and

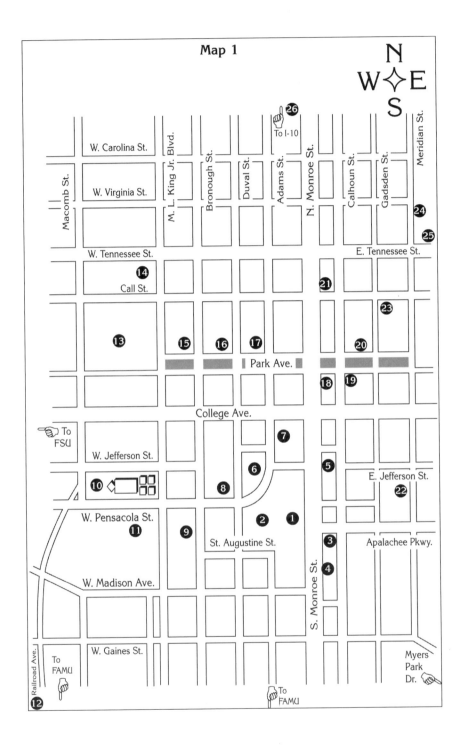

Map 1

Map 1. Tallahassee

1. Old Capitol
2. New Capitol
3. Union Bank
4. Vietnam Veterans' Memorial
5. Leon County Courthouse
6. Tallahassee City Hall
7. Old Downtown Tallahassee
8. Odyssey Science Center and Museum of Art/Tallahassee
9. Museum of Florida History
10. FSU College of Law
11. Tallahassee–Leon County Civic Center
12. Old Railroad Station and Railroad Square
13. Old City Cemetery
14. Murat Graves, St. John's Episcopal Cemetery
15. St. James Church Building
16. The Columns
17. First Presbyterian Church
18. David S. Walker Library
19. Knott House Museum
20. Lewis House on Park Avenue
21. St. John's Episcopal Church
22. Riley House Museum of African American History and Culture
23. LeMoyne Art Foundation
24. Brokaw-McDougall House
25. Leon High School
26. Governor's Mansion

enjoy the diversity of commercial architecture that still evokes an earlier time (before shopping meant driving to the mall).

As agricultural patterns changed, the huge cotton plantations that had supported the elegant social and economic life of Tallahassee were broken up or sold to wealthy northerners such as Alfred Maclay, who turned them into hunting preserves or botanical gardens. In addition to the justly famous Maclay Gardens north of town, Goodwood Museum and Gardens merits a visit. Here you can admire the native and exotic plantings that have made Tallahassee, especially in the springtime, one of the state's most exquisite and colorful attractions.

Tallahassee today offers a bountiful, year-round banquet of cultural charms: art museums such as the LeMoyne Art Foundation and the new Art Museum/Tallahassee; the premiere Museum of Florida History in the R. A. Gray Building; the new Odyssey Science Center in the heart of downtown; and a walk on the wild side through a north Florida forest inhabited by panthers, bears, and wolves at the Tallahassee Museum of History and Natural Science. There are offbeat things to see, too, such as ancient trees turned into dolphins; a country store right out of a Faulkner novel, fixed in time; or a hauntingly beautiful cemetery where all barriers to class and caste have been put to rest.

Enjoy Tallahassee at your leisure, treating the "old town" with due respect, never forgetting that it takes a gracious plenty of time to learn the secrets of a Southern soul.

Old Capitol

Location: South Monroe Street at Apalachee Parkway
Open: Monday–Friday 9–4:30, Saturday 10:30–4:30,
Sunday 12:30–4:30

The red-and-white-striped awnings shading the windows of the restored 1902 capitol are a reminder of the need to protect offices from the fierce Florida sun in the days before air-conditioning. The classical-style building is now a museum of

Old Capitol

Florida's governmental history, and one of the city's most popular attractions. For a while during the 1970s the future of the building was in doubt, as some wanted to demolish it when the new twenty-two-story capitol building was constructed. But preservationists won the day, and the venerable building was returned to its early-twentieth-century appearance, inside and out. The chambers of the Florida Senate, House of Representatives, and Supreme Court contain precise replicas of the original furnishings, and the office of Governor William Sherman Jennings, who led the state in 1902, has been recreated down to the smallest detail, based on old photographs. Lively exhibits and artifacts document the colorful events of Florida's political past in rooms that once served as offices for the state's early leaders. Be sure to notice the careful restoration of the colored glass in the dome of the capitol, and walk down the broad central stairway to see the changing exhibits in the art gallery on the lower level.

New Capitol

Location: South Duval Street, west of the Old Capitol
Open: Monday–Friday 8–5

The towering modern skyscraper that is the present Florida capitol rises twenty-two stories, a highly visible component of the Tallahassee skyline. It was designed by New York architect Edward Durrell Stone and dedicated in 1978. For a free tour of the building, assemble at the plaza-level Tallahassee Area Visitor Information Center. When the legislature is in session, visitors may sit in the galleries of the Senate and House of Representatives and watch their lawmakers at work. In all the offices and hallways are paintings, etchings, and photographs by Florida artists. Slip into the small chapel on the first floor and savor the serenity of a room designed for prayer, meditation, and contemplation. Dedicated in 1980, the chapel, which incorporates natural materials unique to the state, honors the diversity of

New Capitol

Florida's religious heritage. Pause at the center of the rotunda to admire the huge state seal, surrounded by smaller seals representing the foreign powers that once ruled Florida. Then take the elevator to the top floor and enjoy a panoramic view of the seven hills upon which the capital city is built. Also on the twenty-second floor is the Capitol Gallery, which features changing exhibits of the works of distinguished Florida artists. The west plaza of the capitol faces the Florida Supreme Court, and the spacious, paved plaza on the east that connects the old and new capitols is often the site of festive events.

Union Bank

Location: 219 Calhoun Street at Apalachee Parkway
Open: Monday–Friday 9–4

Built for wealthy plantation owners in 1841, this small temple of finance served after the Civil War as a Freedman's Bureau bank for former slaves. Through the years the building was also used, among other things, as a feed store, shoe factory, and dance studio. It was moved to its present site across from the Old

Union Bank Building

Capitol and restored to its 1841 appearance in the 1970s. It now serves as the Capitol Complex extension of the Florida Black Archives, displaying artifacts and documents that celebrate Florida's rich African-American heritage. On view are collections on blacks in entertainment and the military, the Cannonball Adderly Music Collection, Florida A&M University memorabilia, and a Harlem Renaissance collection. The Florida Black Archives, initiated in 1971, were first collected and displayed at the Carnegie Library on the FAMU campus. After more than 150 years of service to the community, the Union Bank has been selected as a research center and museum to present selected items from the extensive holdings of this important collection.

Vietnam Veterans' Memorial

Location: South Monroe Street, across from the Old Capitol

A huge American flag suspended between twin dark gray polished stone towers moves in the breeze, reminding passersby of Florida's casualties and those missing in action in Vietnam. The dramatic memorial, designed by James Kolb of Sarasota and dedicated in 1985, honors the 386,000 Floridians who served in the Vietnam War between 1964 and 1975. It is inscribed with the names of almost 1,942 men and women who died in the Vietnam conflict and the names of the 83 Floridians who are still

Vietnam Veterans' Memorial

listed as "missing in action." A biblical quote from Isaiah, " ... neither shall they learn war any more," is also chiseled into the surface of one of the pylons. Tangible symbols of courage such as medals and everyday objects such as a GI can opener were placed inside the monument as it was being constructed, and visitors to the landscaped plaza may still find poignant mementos, American flags, or flowers placed at the base of the monument.

Leon County Courthouse

Location: Monroe and Jefferson Streets

Leon County Courthouse

The new Leon County Courthouse joined the governmental center of Tallahassee in 1989 to become part of the visual dialogue between the old and new state capitols, the seat of county government, and the city hall. It is situated on Washington Square, one of the city's original public squares and the site of the county courthouse since the 1880s. Leon County was established in 1824 and is named for Spanish explorer Juan Ponce de León. The architectural style of the very modern county government building reflects the neoclassical tradition so pervasive in the state capital. Loggias, grand stairways, columns, and atriums are frequently seen, and a three-story rotunda echoes those in the capitol buildings. Within the building are ten courtrooms, the county commission chamber, and a wide variety of offices that serve the public's needs. Colossal live oaks, preserved by placing the building well back on its site, provide a dynamic contrast to the formal, geometrical massing of the building. The imposing, smooth-textured building, in green, brown, and white hues, blends in well with the trees and sky.

Tallahassee City Hall

Location: Jefferson and Adams Streets

The dark-brick Tallahassee City Hall with its rosy marble entrance was completed in 1983 on the site of Wayne Square, one of five squares set aside for public use in the 1825 Tallahassee city plan. A traditional, neoclassical-style city hall stood on the site until it was demolished in 1981. The new city hall has a graceful inner curve breaking the severe lines of its facade, which relates to the swelling outline of a section of the Leon County Courthouse facing it one block east on Jefferson Street. This interior curve forms an expansive, semicircular lobby that welcomes visitors to the building. A grand stairway leads to the second-floor gallery where displays of art are exhibited on walls and balconies, illuminated with natural light that pours in

Tallahassee City Hall

through large windows. The Tallahassee City Hall is located between the state capitol buildings and old downtown Tallahassee.

Old Downtown Tallahassee

Location: Monroe, Jefferson, and Adams Streets

The commercial hub of Tallahassee, its central business district, has always been affected by its proximity to the capitol and other government buildings, yet it has served the needs of the townspeople as well. For more than 160 years downtown Tallahassee has seen a changing array of hotels, restaurants, entertainment spots, meeting places, banks, stores, and office buildings. An eclectic architectural ensemble, with some of the buildings dating back to the nineteenth century, still brings vivacity and variety to the revitalized downtown. Many of the vintage brick

Monroe Street, Old Downtown Tallahassee

buildings that reflect so much of Tallahassee history, such as Gallie's Hall with its decorative iron posts and railing on a corner lot across from City Hall, have been adapted to modern uses, and new buildings have been designed to harmonize with the small scale and Southern charm of the city. Inviting streetscapes, especially on Adams Street with its outdoor cafés, seasonal landscaping, and pedestrian-friendly atmosphere, draw the public and private buildings together, blending the old with the new.

Odyssey Science Center and Museum of Art/Tallahassee

Location: 350 South Duval Street
Open: Tuesday–Saturday 1–5, Sunday 1–5

In the heart of downtown Tallahassee, anchoring the south-west corner of Kleman Park, is a new museum center with a dual design. Two floors of the bold, modern, blue-and-gray building bring the world of interactive science to the capital city, and the third floor is devoted to exhibitions of works of art. Nearly ten years in the making, this cultural center will engage, entertain, and inspire people of all ages. Enter the circular lobby and be surrounded by exciting sights and sounds where art and science collaborate and invigorate all the senses. Frequently changing displays and hand-on exhibits offer kaleidoscopic opportunities to view the complementary worlds of art and science in a friendly setting. Visit Odyssey Science Center online at www.odyssey-

Odyssey Science Center and Museum of Art/Tallahassee

sciencecenter.org to learn more about the permanent exhibits and schedules for traveling exhibits.

Museum of Florida History

Location: Ground floor of the R. A. Gray Building,
500 South Bronough Street
Open: Monday–Friday 9–4:30, Saturday 10–4:30,
Sunday 12–4:30

F lorida's past is preserved, exhibited, and interpreted here in a plethora of intriguing displays: mastodon bones, Native American pottery, sunken Spanish treasure, a reconstructed river steamer, a 1920s' "tin-can tourist" camper, a citrus-packing house, and other sidelights that bring our everyday and extraordi-

Museum of Florida History

nary history to life. Browse through the museum's changing exhibits, which may feature quilts one month and Florida architecture the next, and the fascinating memorabilia and artifacts from the museum's vast collection that are showcased in a special gallery. Some of the exhibits assembled in the state's official history museum will travel throughout Florida, a stimulating and constantly changing road show featuring the people and events that make Florida's history unique.

Tallahassee–Leon County Civic Center

Location: 505 West Pensacola Street

Tallahassee–Leon County Civic Center

T he pivotal location of the Civic Center, within blocks of both the FSU and FAMU campuses as well as the Tallahassee government and business core, contributes to its impact on the community. Both universities hold their commencement ceremonies here, and sports events such as FSU basketball games draw large crowds. The multipurpose convention and entertainment center, which opened in 1981, also hosts concerts and a Broadway show series and is equipped to present ice shows and hockey games. The boldly sloping red-brick walls create an angular configuration, the high pitch of the roof accommodates a soaring 119-foot ceiling in the interior arena, and terraces and open spaces shaded by louvered concrete covers expand the outdoor use of the facility.

Old Railroad Station and Railroad Square

Location: 918 Railroad Avenue and McDonnell Avenue

Old Railroad Station

The Old Seaboard Coastline Railroad Station has been around since 1858. As an Amtrak station, it is one of the oldest active passenger train terminals in Florida. Renovated to retain some of its distinctive features and given a trendy paint job in recent years, the prominent brick structure is a historical link with the first Florida railroad, a primitive mule-drawn conveyance that connected Tallahassee to St. Marks on the Gulf coast. The old abandoned rail bed is now a popular sixteen-mile paved "rails-to-trails" recreational corridor. Around the corner from the old station is Railroad Square, an enclave of dozens of artists' studios tucked into an industrial park on the other side of the tracks. Professional artists have installed massive welded-steel sculptures in the parklike entrance to the Square, and gourmet coffees and goodies are sold in an old railroad car converted into a café.

Old City Cemetery

Location: Entrance on Martin Luther King Jr.
Boulevard near Park Avenue

In 1829 the legislative council and the city fathers of Tallahassee wanted to make sure their public burying ground was located far from the center of town to protect the health of its citizens. Now the four-block-square Old City Cemetery, one of the capital city's most singular historic sites, is practically in the center of Tallahassee. It is one of the most democratic gathering places in the city as well. Here are the final resting places of governors and carpenters, slaves and their masters, ministers and outlaws, Union soldiers and Confederate veterans, stillborn infants and victims of yellow fever epidemics. As you wander among the graves—some bearing simple stone markers engraved with just names and dates, others elaborate Victorian creations with sentimental verses and carved images—it is easy to believe in tales of ghostly apparitions, especially on a gloomy day with the wind moaning through the cedar trees and twisting the heavy strands of gray Spanish moss in the ancient live

Old City Cemetery

oak trees. An informative brochure available to visitors at the entrance provides a wealth of information about the cemetery and those who are laid to rest here.

Murat Graves, St. John's Episcopal Cemetery

Location: Call Street and Martin Luther King Jr. Boulevard

They stand united in the tree-shaded St. John's Episcopal Cemetery: twin majestic, obelisk-shaped monuments on a raised platform, marking the graves of Prince Achille Murat and his Virginia-born wife, Princess Catherine Willis Murat. How this royal couple came to be buried in Tallahassee is both a roman-

Murat Graves, St. John's Episcopal Cemetery

tic saga and a frontier legend. Achille Murat (1801–1847) was the son of Napoleon Bonaparte's sister Maria and Joachim Murat, one of Napoleon's favorite generals. Catherine Willis Murat (1803–1867) also had distinguished relatives. Her mother was the granddaughter of Betty Washington, sister of George Washington. The Willis family had moved to Florida in the early 1820s and settled in Tallahassee. A young widow by 1826, Catherine met Murat, who had found his way to Florida following the death of his father and the exile of his family, in the aftermath of Napoleon's fallen empire. Achille and Catherine married and moved into a log house on his plantation but set the finest style, serving their guests with golden utensils and napkins marked with the Napoleonic crest. To learn more about the Murats, visit the Tallahassee Museum of History and Natural Science and tour Bellevue, the home the captivating Catherine Murat bought after her husband's death from typhoid fever in 1847.

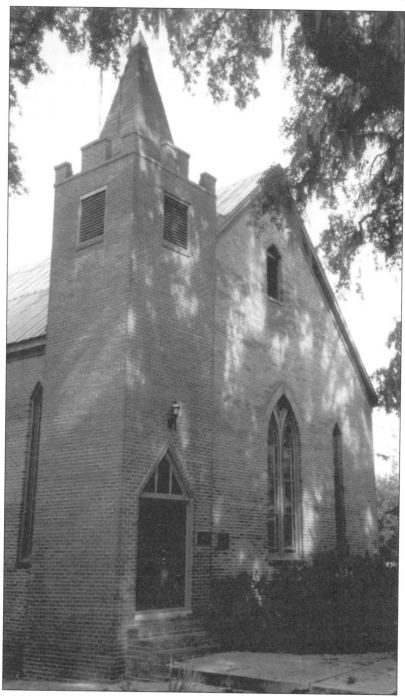

St. James Church Building

St. James Church Building

Location: Bronough Street and Park Avenue

This sturdy red-brick Gothic-revival church was built in 1899 by the Christian Methodist Episcopal congregation. Among the members of the church, which sprang from the Trinity Methodist Episcopal Church formed in the 1820s, were some of the most prominent members of Tallahassee's black community, including trustee John Gilmore Riley, a successful businessman and educator. When the St. James CME congregation moved to a new building, the interior of this one was remodeled; it is now used as an office. However, the traditional Gothic character of the building has been preserved in the well-shaped front window, the narrow lancet windows at the sides set with tinted glass, and the crenelated roofline of the square bell tower.

The Columns

Location: Park Avenue and Duval Street

The oldest building in Tallahassee, built in 1830 as a home for a wealthy banker with the easy-to-remember name of William "Money" Williams, continues to welcome visitors with Southern style and grace. The Columns, so named for the four ponderous columns in its portico, is now the headquarters of the Tallahassee Area Chamber of Commerce. The three-story, classical-style brick building on the corner of Park Avenue and Duval Street has served as a bank, doctor's office, and boarding house, as well as a fashionable residence. A popular restaurant called the Dutch Kitchen occupied the basement area until 1956. The building was moved to its present location in the 1970s, but it has lost none of its original dignity and elegance. It is sumptuously decorated and furnished in period antiques, and a pair of statues of friendly dogs poses winsomely at the entrance.

The Columns

First Presbyterian Church

Location: Park Avenue and Adams Street

W hen Tallahassee was chosen as the capital of the new Territory of Florida in 1824, one of the first acts of the legislative council was to appoint a chaplain. The Reverend Henry White, a Presbyterian minister, was given permission to preach each Sunday in the capitol building, which was as yet unfinished. In 1838 the Presbyterians completed the construction of their brick Greek-revival-style church, which they financed through the sale of pews. Slaves who attended sat in a gallery reserved for their use and were admitted as members of the church.

First Presbyterian Church

The original bell still hangs in the lofty steeple, one of the few that survived the Civil War–era practice of donating church bells to the Confederacy to be made into cannons. In the 1890s, Methodist as well as Presbyterian services were held here: the neighborly Presbyterians offered the use of their church on alternate Sundays while the new Methodist church was under construction. Although the original rectangular windows and doors have been replaced by those in the neo-Gothic style, the First Presbyterian Church on Adams Street still stands, the oldest church and the oldest public building in the city.

David S. Walker Library

Location: 209 East Park Avenue

David S. Walker Library

One of Tallahassee's early-twentieth-century showplaces was its library, named for David S. Walker, governor of Florida from 1865 to 1868. Walker, a staunch champion of education, later served as a circuit judge and was the founder of the Florida University Library Association. The first home of the private subscription library was in the second story of an adjacent office building owned by Walker. The Walker family donated assets for the new building, and additional funds were raised with proceeds from bazaars and theatrical productions. The red-brick structure, a Tallahassee landmark since its construction in 1903, is a delightful example of neoclassical-revival architecture. The Walker Library, one of the oldest in the state, was also a Tallahassee social and cultural center for many years. The gentry used the balcony as a game room, and collectors displayed their prize specimens and curios on the shelves that were not filled with books and magazines. The Walker Library, which still has its historic interior woodwork and bookcases crammed with old volumes, was replaced by a new public library in the 1950s. It is now the home of Springtime Tallahassee, Inc., which organizes the annual seasonal festival that celebrates the history, culture, and beauty of the city.

Knott House Museum

Location 301 East Park Avenue
Open: Wednesday–Friday 1–3, Saturday 10–3

Known as "The House that Rhymes," this time capsule of Tallahassee history is located in the Park Avenue Historic District. The antebellum mansion, built in 1843, holds a prominent place in the city's history. It may have been built by George Proctor, a free black man who constructed many of the grand early homes in Tallahassee. The Emancipation Proclamation, freeing the slaves of north Florida, was read from the front steps on May 20, 1865, by Union General Edward McCook, who occupied the house after the Civil War. In 1929 it was acquired by

Knott House Museum

William V. Knott, former state treasurer, comptroller, and auditor, and an unsuccessful candidate for governor. Mrs. Luella Knott, his wife, was a musician and poet. She tied her whimsical poems, printed on little cards, to many of the home's Victorian-style furnishings, delighting her guests and today's visitors to this friendly and charming house museum.

Lewis House on Park Avenue

Location: 316 East Park Avenue

B. C. Lewis, a Yankee transplant to Tallahassee in the 1830s, founded a banking dynasty that made a lasting impression on the business and social life of the state's capital city. The

Lewis House

Lewis family loved giving parties and actively supported the annual May Party, an extravagant pageant held for many years in Lewis Park in front of their house, beneath the venerable May Oak (which stood until 1986). Lewis Park, one of Tallahassee's first public parks, was created and maintained by Captain William Lewis at his own expense in the 1880s. The historic Lewis house, built in the 1840s, today is an excellent example of adaptive reuse, the fate of many of the fine older homes in Tallahassee's Park Avenue Historic District. As the residential character of the neighborhood has changed, the houses have become offices for organizations, associations, and professionals. The Lewis home is now the headquarters of the Florida Council for Community Mental Health. The new owners have restored the house with its Victorian turret, broad porches, and fine interior woodwork.

St. John's Episcopal Church

Location: 211 South Monroe Street

Brilliant colors from the narrow, stained-glass windows pattern the interior of the neo-Gothic-style church built in 1880 for the city's oldest Episcopal congregation, and the hand-hewn beams of the hammer-beam ceiling create intricate designs against the white plaster. The magnificent edifice with its square tower and artistic brickwork replaced a wooden church built in 1838 that burned in 1879. Twenty of the original nineteenth-century windows are still in place, a harmonious blend of lacelike etching and rich glowing colors. One commemorates the Civil War battle of Shiloh on April 6, 1862. The altar screen carved from native woods by a local artisan is another treasure of reverent creativity. Visitors to the busy heart of Tallahassee may enjoy St. John's serene inner garden with its fountain and statues, created by the wraparound buildings of the school and the smaller, newer chapel on the south side.

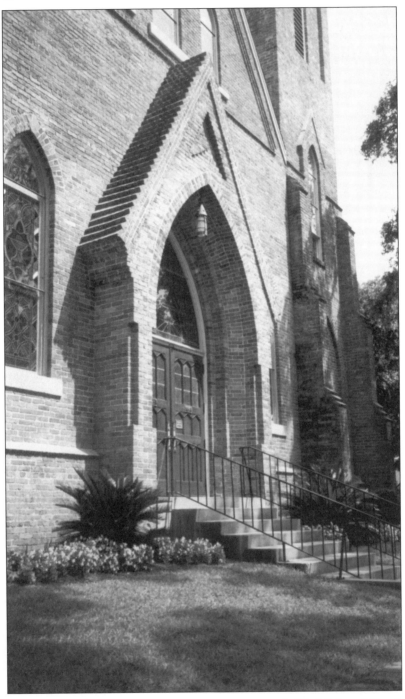

St. John's Episcopal Church

Riley House Museum of African American History and Culture

Location: 419 East Jefferson Street
Open: Monday, Wednesday, and Friday 10–4

The two-story home of John Gilmore Riley, civic leader, successful businessman, and principal of Lincoln Academy, the city's first public school for African Americans, has been restored and is now a delightful house museum. Some rooms in the 1890s house, which was the center of a small, middle-class black neighborhood located close to the capitol building, display Riley family furnishings. But the colorfully painted house with its encircling porches is also a center for research and study. It features interesting exhibits related to the history of the African Americans of Tallahassee and Leon County, from Reconstruction through the Civil Rights movement.

Riley House

LeMoyne Art Foundation

Location: 125 South Gadsden Street
Open: Tuesday–Saturday 10–5, Sunday 1–5

Located in the Park Avenue Historic District, the LeMoyne has been the city's center for the visual arts for more than thirty years. It is named for Jacques LeMoyne de Morgues, a member of a sixteenth-century French expedition to Florida and the first artist known to have visited the New World. Exhibits from the museum's permanent collection of works by Florida artists alternate with stimulating and innovative thematic shows. Lectures, gallery talks, and musical evenings are presented to the public in conjunction with exhibitions. At the rear of the main building, the 1854 Meginnis-Munroe House, is the Helen Lind Sculpture Garden, a popular place for receptions and other social events. The LeMoyne has expanded to encompass several adjacent buildings. The Munroe House next door welcomes visitors to a delightful museum shop; other buildings offer art education activities for students of all ages.

The Meginnis-Munroe House, part of the LeMoyne Art Foundation

Brokaw-McDougall House

Location: 329 North Meridian Street
Open: Monday–Friday 8–5

Peres Bonney Brokaw, a prosperous livery stable owner who also served in the state legislature and the Confederate cavalry, built this Classical revival-style mansion with Italianate features in 1856. His daughter married a Scotsman, Alexander McDougall, and the strikingly fashionable two-story house remained in the Brokaw-McDougall family until the 1970s. The site is distinguished by the stately live oak trees, planted by Peres Brokaw, and the formal gardens, which were restored as a bicentennial project of the Florida Federation of Garden Clubs. When it was built the house was on the outskirts of town, which gives us an idea of how small the state capital was in the 1850s. It is

Brokaw-McDougall House

one of the finest remaining antebellum residences in Tallahassee. With its elegant period furnishings and decorations, it is a favorite place for parties, meetings, and receptions.

Leon High School

Location: 550 East Tennessee Street

Seldom do public high school buildings command the majestic position that Leon High School occupies overlooking terraced playing fields, and seldom do they resemble Italian-renaissance palaces. Designed by M. Leo Elliott of Tampa, one of Florida's most prominent architects, the home of the Leon Lions was built in the Mediterranean-revival style in the mid-1930s during

Leon High School

the Depression, partly with federal funds. It is now listed in the National Register of Historic Places, thanks to the work of an LHS student. A ruddy barrel-tile roof spreads over the massive three-story brick structure, which is ornamented with a broad frieze of colored terra-cotta tile, classical panels with winged angel motifs, wrought-iron railings, and decorative tile water fountains.

Governor's Mansion

Location: 700 North Adams Street, ten blocks north of the Capitol

Until 1907, Florida's governors had to purchase or rent a home in the state capital. But that year Governor Napoleon Bonaparte Broward moved into the new mansion, designed by Jacksonville architect Henry John Klutho in the neoclassical style with no fewer than twenty-four huge columns

Florida's Finest *at the Governor's Mansion*

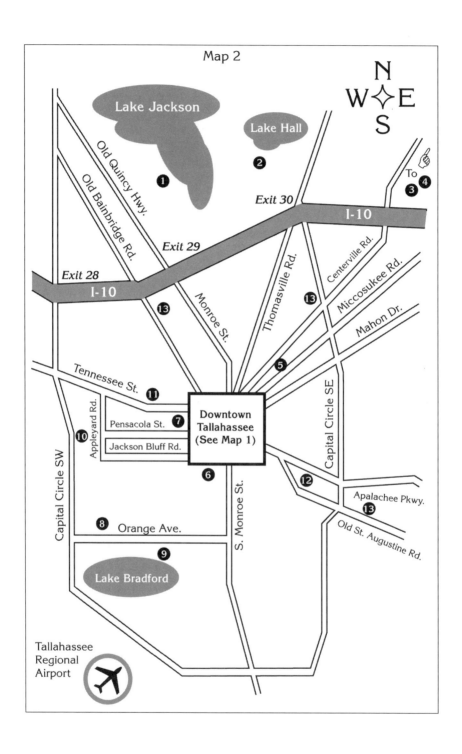

Map 2

Map 2. Tallahassee Area

1. Lake Jackson Mounds State Archaeological Site
2. Alfred B. Maclay State Gardens
3. Old Pisgah United Methodist Church
4. Bradley's Store
5. Goodwood Museum and Gardens
6. Florida Agricultural and Mechanical University
7. Florida State University
8. Innovation Park, National High Magnetic Field Laboratory, and FAMU/FSU School of Engineering
9. Tallahassee Museum of History and Natural Science
10. Tallahassee Community College
11. Mission San Luis de Apalachee
12. Tallahassee Chain-Saw Art
13. Canopy Roads

in front. By the 1950s, "this old house" was too small and in need of costly repairs, so it was demolished and the present mansion built on the same site. In 1957 Governor LeRoy Collins and his family, who had resided temporarily next door at The Grove, the ancestral home of First Lady Mary Call Collins, moved into the new mansion. Its facade resembles that of The Hermitage, the Tennessee home of Andrew Jackson, Florida's first territorial governor. Antique furnishings and works of art on loan from the Ringling Museum of Art in Sarasota embellish the formal, public rooms on the first floor, while the private rooms for the governor's family are on the second floor. Landscaping for the home of the state's First Family includes many native plants and trees, and a small public park has been created in front of the mansion where visitors can enjoy the delightful statue of children at play, created by Tallahassee sculptor Stanley "Sandy" Proctor. Called *Florida's Finest*, it symbolizes the hope of Florida's future.

Lake Jackson Mounds State Archaeological Site

Location: 2 miles north of I-10 on US 27, turn right on Crowder Road,
2 miles to park entrance at 3600 Indian Mound Road
Open: Daily 8–sundown

S tanding on the hand-built earthen mound, hickory nuts underfoot and shade filtering through the overarching trees, try to reach back in time almost a thousand years. Imagine overlooking cleared fields tilled by the Lake Jackson people and seeing other mounds in the near distance, some of them topped with the homes of the tribe's elite, one crowned by a ceremonial lodge with smoke lazily climbing upward from the opening in the roof. Six of these mounds, one with steps leading to its summit, are all that remain of the Native American settlement that flourished on Lake Jackson between A.D. 1200 and A.D. 1500, now the site of a state

Lake Jackson Mounds State Archaelogical Site

archaeological site and park. For reasons unknown, the people abandoned this auspicious location and moved away before de Soto and his Spanish troops came through the area in 1539. The Lake Jackson Mounds State Archaeological Site is protected yet accessible, a state park with picnic areas and outdoor interpretive exhibits that reveal the known details of this mysterious place. A meandering nature trail leads to the Butler Mill site where eighteenth-century settlers ground corn into meal, a skill the Lake Jackson people would have appreciated.

Alfred B. Maclay State Gardens

Location: 1 mile north of I-10 on US 319 to
entrance at 3540 Thomasville Road
Open: Daily 8–sundown

I n the peak of the blooming season, from January through April, visitors can witness a continuous pageant of floral beauty as hundreds of camellias, azaleas, dogwoods, and redbuds show their colors. Developed as a southern retreat by New Yorker Alfred B. Maclay in the 1920s, the property was deeded to the state by his

Maclay Gardens

Maclay House

widow in the 1950s, when it was known as Killearn Gardens. Native plants and exotic species blend perfectly in the landscape, which features views of Lake Hall, pathways leading to the Secret Garden and the Reflecting Pool, and nature trails through the forested park. The Maclay House is also open during the blooming season, a charming getaway cottage set like a jewel on a velvet green lawn.

Old Pisgah United Methodist Church

Location: Centerville Road, 10 miles northeast of Tallahassee, turn at Pisgah Church Road

G ather the quiet simplicity of the Old Pisgah Church about you like a blessing as you enter the high-ceilinged sanctuary filled with light from the long windows on either side.

Old Pisgah United Methodist Church: exterior (top) and interior (bottom)

The oldest Methodist church in Leon County wears its age gracefully. It was organized in 1830 as a Methodist Episcopal congregation for the Centerville community and was once one of the leading churches in middle Florida. The present sanctuary was built in 1858 on seven acres of land donated by the Felkel family. The simple but elegant Greek-revival-style church with its hand-hewn boxed pews and galleries still fills with worshipers each Sunday. Take a stroll through the cemetery, its monuments and markers graced with wildflowers and shaded by ancient trees. Here are buried, in unmarked graves, many in the Centerville community who fell victim to the yellow fever epidemic that raged through the land in 1841.

Bradley's Store

Location: Centerville Road, 15 miles northeast of Tallahassee

Continue down Centerville Road to Moccasin Gap Road for a taste of old-fashioned country commerce. Bradley's Store, which has been selling groceries since 1927, still offers customers red licorice ropes and peppermint sticks, rubber boots and tin pails, jars of pickles and fresh vegetables, canned goods, home-cured sausage made from Grandma Bradley's secret recipe, and bottles of cane syrup prepared on the grounds. If you are there at the right time of the year—late fall—you may be able to watch the old-fashioned cane-grinding operation. The modest, one-story frame store with a tin roof and sides has two gas pumps in front and old signs and advertisements tacked to the walls. If you want a relaxing interlude, settle down in one of the old rocking chairs out on the open front porch and watch the sun filtering through the branches of the huge oak trees or admire the cows in the pasture across the road. Bradley's Store is the genuine thing, certified as historically significant by its listing in the National Register of Historic Places.

Bradley's Store

Goodwood Museum and Gardens

Location: 1600 Miccosukee Road
Open: Monday–Friday 9–5

The history of Goodwood merges with the history of Florida: a number of prominent former owners made significant contributions to the state's social and political history. This nineteen-acre showplace, formerly part of a much larger nineteenth-century cotton and corn plantation, is being restored to its former glory as the glamorous heart of Tallahassee social life. In the process, much is being learned about the tastes, lifestyles, and activities of those who have lived at Goodwood. The grounds, with their stately live oak trees and heirloom flower gardens, are open to visitors, and the elegant 1840s mansion and outbuildings are being restored to once more graciously welcome the

Goodwood Museum and Gardens

public. This exciting work-in-progress promises to delight and intrigue all who relish the revitalization of historic homes and gardens.

Florida Agricultural and Mechanical University (FAMU)

Location: between Adams Street and Wahnish Way

S pread over the crest of one of Tallahassee's highest hills is the attractive campus of Florida A&M University. Founded in 1887 as the State Normal School for Colored Students to prepare African-American teachers for Florida's public schools, the state-supported, land-grant institution became Florida Agricultural and Mechanical College in 1909 and attained university status in 1953. The historic Carnegie Library, home of the Florida Black Archives, has recently been refurbished, as have most of the classical Georgian-style classrooms, administrative buildings, and residence halls built earlier in the century. Contemporary architectural designs of newer academic and research facilities complement the traditional campus plan. FAMU is proud of its world-class "Marching 100" band and the powerhouse Rattlers football team. It is highly ranked as one of the nation's top historically black universities, earning *Time* magazine's and Princeton Review's College of the Year awards in 1997.

FAMU's Lee Hall

National High Magnetic Field Laboratory

Location: 1800 Paul Dirac Drive, Innovation Park

A consortium of research institutions—Florida State University, the University of Florida, and the Los Alamos National Laboratory—collaborated to establish this interdisciplinary research facility, funded in part by the National Science Foundation. Vice President Al Gore spoke at the dedication ceremony in 1994. In addition to the FSU and FAMU faculty members and graduate students who use the NHMFL, scientists come to Tallahassee from all over the world to conduct studies in the highly specialized laboratories within this complex. Notable is the Millikelvin Laboratory, whose superconductivity magnets are capable of probing the basic properties of materials at very low temperatures in high magnetic fields. The NHMFL consists of three main buildings, streamlined and functional in appearance. An abstract sculpture symbolizing the far-reaching possibilities of research conducted here in the biological and physical sciences hangs in the entrance atrium at the center of the complex. Tours of the NHMFL for students in grades K-12 boost their interest in the sciences and encourage their teachers to explore new frontiers in preparing their pupils for the future. Tours of the NHMFL may also be arranged for interested members of the general public. Call 850-644-0850 for more information.

Tallahassee Community College

Location: 444 Appleyard Drive

The campus of Tallahassee Community College sparkles with new buildings and some freshly updated ones that have served the student body since the college's founding in 1966. With an enrollment of more than ten thousand, TCC serves not only its three-county (Leon, Gadsden, and Wakulla) district but also attracts students from other parts of Florida, the nation, and the world. Many TCC graduates transfer to institutions in the state university system such as FSU and FAMU to continue their education, while others who work toward associate of arts or associate of science degrees concentrate on vocational programs. The spacious campus, formerly Dale Mabry Field, a pilot training base during World War II, has been used to good advantage. The James H. Hinson Jr. Administration Building, named for TCC's third president, was built in 1993. Some of the traditional yet timeless architectural features of the prominent brick structure—circular atriums, gables, arches, and columns—are echoed in the adjoining library, student union, and classroom buildings. Cutting-edge technology is also part of TCC's present and future, from the online database resources in the new library to distance-learning courses offered on the Internet. To learn more, turn to the TCC website: www.tallahassee.cc.fl.us.

Tallahassee Community College

Tallahassee Museum of History and Natural Science

Location: 3945 Museum Drive
Open: Monday–Saturday 9–5, Sunday 12:30–5

One of the few museums in the nation that combines historical buildings, displays of native wildlife, contemporary exhibits, and a beautiful natural setting is located on a fifty-two-acre site on a chain of lakes in southwest Tallahassee. Where else can you stroll through an enchanting woodland and see black bears, red wolves, American eagles, and Florida panthers in their native habitats? All the animals in the zoological collection of the Tallahassee Museum of History and Natural Science (formerly the Tallahassee Junior Museum) are native to the state, and the long

Bellevue, Tallahassee Museum of History and Natural Science

boardwalk meandering through the sanctuary gives visitors a unintrusive close-up view of a wide variety of Florida wildlife. How people in the past lived their daily lives in the "Big Bend," a popular designation for this part of the state, is shown in a marvelous collection of buildings, including a late-nineteenth-century Cracker farm, a one-room schoolhouse, a country church, and the home of a princess. The latter, Bellevue, built around 1840, was once owned by Catherine Willis Murat, whose husband Achille was Napoleon's nephew and the son of the king of Naples. There are more surprises in store for visitors to this museum—an exceptional place to take the family, to show visitors from out of town, and to take a break from the fast pace of modern life.

Mission San Luis de Apalachee

Mission San Luis de Apalachee

Location: 2020 West Mission Road
Open: Monday–Friday 9–4:30, Saturday 10–4, Sunday 12–4:30

Layers of history are being peeled back on this hilltop archaeological site that once was the location of a thriving seventeenth-century Spanish mission, a sizable Apalachee village, and a bustling provincial trading center. San Luis was abandoned and burned in 1704 in anticipation of raids by the British and their Creek Indian allies. It became an antebellum plantation and was later a residential estate. The fifty-acre site was purchased by the state in 1983 and has since produced a rich yield in artifacts and archaeological evidence now being used to recreate some of the original buildings: a Spanish residence, the mission church, the Apalachee council house. Interpretive exhibits, guided tours, and living history programs at San Luis bring the everyday experiences of the Spanish pioneers and the Apalachee people to life. Tours begin at the Visitors Center, a brick-and-stone mansion built in the 1930s.

Tallahassee's Chain-Saw Art

Locations: Various

Throughout Tallahassee delightful sculptural creations pop up in surprising places—a trio of leaping dolphins on the verge of a busy roadway, a sunburst lighting up a corner of Myers Park, the face of an ancient and quirky creature on the grounds of the Tallahassee Museum of History and Natural Science. They are the work of John Birch, Tallahassee's chain-saw artist, who turns dead or discarded trees into monumental expressions of his fancy. Some of them, like the dolphins frisking on Old St. Augustine Road, are carved from the dead tree still standing on its original site. Others are moved to likely locations in the Talla-

An example of Tallahassee's chain-saw art

hassee landscape after the artist recycles the massive tree trunks into intriguing images. Many of the chain-saw sculptures are in public places, such as city parks, offering curbside glimpses of the reincarnated forest giants.

Canopy Roads

Locations: Various

One of the most evocative images of the Southern landscape is a narrow road overshadowed by the spreading branches of live oak trees, hung with generous swaths of Spanish moss, standing on either side. Most of the old canopy roads have given way to wide, asphalt-covered highways, the trees pushed back and pruned, if they have been allowed to stand at all. However, leading to and from Tallahassee are more than sixty miles of officially designated and protected roadway, its natural canopy framing some of the country's most scenic byways. Sections of Old St. Augustine Road, Thomasville Road, Miccosukee Road, Centerville Road, and Old Bainbridge Road meander along under the sheltering arms of giant trees interlaced over the road, and thoughtfully placed road signs invite drivers to slow down and savor the journey for its own sweet sake.

Canopy road

Another of Tallahassee's canopy roads

2
FSU

A Historical Sketch of Florida State University

One of Florida's ten state universities, Florida State has an enrollment of more than thirty thousand undergraduate and graduate students. It is a major research institution with outstanding faculty and programs in the humanities and sciences. FSU is nationally recognized in the visual and performing arts, and its seventeen athletic teams, members of the Atlantic Coast Conference, are highly ranked in national competition.

It also has one of the most beautiful campuses, particularly in the spring when the dogwoods, azaleas, and camellias are in bloom. Towering pines, noble oak trees, and grassy quadrangles set off an eclectic ensemble of buildings with a history spanning almost one hundred years.

In a foreword to *Seminole History*, famous FSU alum Burt Reynolds expressed it well:"... the red bricks, the ivy and moss of the trees—it was exactly what I thought a university should be." For generations, students arriving for the first time have felt the same thing, that the FSU campus fits the image of Yale or Harvard or Princeton and must have been there forever. Not quite, but since 1855 a school devoted to higher education has stood on this high point overlooking the "old town" of Tallahassee.

As the state's oldest active university site, the crest of this hill has seen many changes. At the urging of Mayor Francis Eppes, Thomas Jefferson's grandson, the city built College Hall here in the 1850s in a successful bid to persuade the legislature to establish the West Florida Seminary in Tallahassee. By the 1880s, the school had not only survived the hard years of the Civil War but rebounded as a coeducational institution with an expanding curriculum. Under the leadership of President Albert A. Murphree, it was renamed Florida State College in 1901, a four-year institution of higher learning offering both bachelor's and master's degrees. The next year the FSC football team made a creditable showing in its first intercollegiate season, including a hometown win over arch-rival Florida Agricultural College of Lake City, which changed its name to the University of Florida the following year.

Despite some opposition from the Tallahassee contingent, in 1905 the Florida legislature passed the Buckman Act, which closed several small colleges and seminaries and replaced them with a university for men and a college for women. These two, plus the Normal School for Negroes in Tallahassee and the School for the Deaf and Blind in St. Augustine, were placed under one Board of Control. The university was to be in Gainesville and would be called the University of Florida. Florida State College in Tallahassee became Florida Female College, a name that was changed in 1909 to Florida State College for Women, or FSCW.

There was little enthusiasm among the Florida legislators concerning college education for women: some considered it a bit scandalous and others a waste of money. So President Murphree had a tough time securing funds to continue the academic and athletic programs he had established at FSC. The campus covered about thirteen acres and had only three buildings and a makeshift gymnasium. When Murphree was appointed president of UF in 1909, he was succeeded by Dr. Edward Conradi, who served as president of FSCW for the next thirty-two years. By the time of Conradi's retirement in 1941, enrollment had risen from 257 to 2,000, and the campus had expanded to more than 700 acres, including a farm and dairy and Camp Flastacowo (Seminole Reservation) on Lake Bradford.

Two overcrowded wooden buildings housed the students and did double duty as dining hall and classrooms. When one burned in 1906, it was replaced by Bryan Hall, still standing in all its Gothic splendor. Bryan soon became the social center of campus, with a spacious and refined parlor and a sunken garden in front where outdoor events were held.

To foster school spirit and a sense of comradeship, groups called the Odds and Evens, based on class years, were organized in 1912. Thus began the tradition at FSCW of odd-numbered classes challenging even-numbered classes in athletic and other displays of skill and talent. Sporting events were fiercely contested, original plays were produced, and each class competed in an effort to leave its distinctive mark on the campus. The Odd-Even rivalry, which reached a fever pitch each Thanksgiving when the basketball teams competed, extended even to the donation of class gifts such as the entrance gates and the fountain in front of the Westcott Building.

In 1910 the old College Hall, like a pitcher that had cracked one time too many to be repaired again, was replaced by the new Administration Building (Westcott). In addition to offices and classrooms, it had a one-thousand-seat auditorium, complete with an organ and a grand piano.

More and more young women applied for admission to FSCW, and a new brick dormitory was built north of Bryan Hall to accommodate the new students. Reynolds Hall opened in 1913, and soon the students had a new dining hall with grand, high ceilings reminiscent of English university refectories. "Dining room girls" waited on tables in exchange for room and board and had to maintain high grades to keep up their "dining room scholarships."

William Edwards, the architect of the Board of Control, designed the new red-brick campus buildings in the Tudor or late-Gothic style, characterized by a broad pointed arch, crenelated parapets and towers, and stone decorations. Edwards, who also designed buildings for the University of Florida and Florida A&M University, managed to provide flexible structures within the budget allotted to him, buildings that created an immediate feeling of strength and stability. This architectural legacy, as Burt Reynolds recalled, made the campus look exactly as a university should look. In the mid-1920s Edwards was succeeded by Rudolph Weaver, who continued the traditional architectural approach throughout the 1930s.

During World War I two new buildings were constructed: a dorm called Broward Hall, and the Education Building (later renamed the Psychology Building), the first building on campus designed exclusively for academic purposes. In 1922 and 1923 a second academic building, Science Hall (the Diffenbaugh Building), was built south of the Administration Building. The long-awaited library (Dodd Hall) was erected in two stages in the 1920s, designed by Rudolph Weaver in the most exuberant expression of the Gothic style possible. Its lavishly decorated entrance, paneled lobby, and reading room with massive carved ceiling beams were a tribute to the growing reputation for academic excellence that FSCW enjoyed.

In one of the shrewdest deals of the 1920s Florida land boom, business manager John Gabriel Kellum acquired a large swath of property west of the main campus, up to what is now Woodward Avenue. He turned much of it into a productive farm and dairy to supply the dining room with fresh vegetables, eggs, and milk. Kellum was also astute enough to pick up some waterfront acreage on Lake Bradford as a recreation area for the students, who happily walked the five miles to the rustic camp for picnics and water sports.

In 1922, a fourth residence hall was built north of Reynolds Hall. It was named for a Tallahassee girl, Jennie Henderson, who had graduated from Florida State College and later married its former president, Albert A. Murphree. Gilchrist Hall, built between 1926 and 1928, moved FSCW in a westerly direction and somewhat relieved a drastic shortage of campus housing. By the time Gilchrist Hall was fully occupied, more than eleven hundred women lived on campus, with more than five hundred additional students living at home, in sorority houses, or in off-campus housing.

The History Building (Williams Building) was built in the late 1920s and expanded as funds became available. At most times, President Conradi's requests for newer and larger facilities met with stiff resistance from the legislature and Board of Control. A great deal of patience and persistence were required to secure appropriations for the growing college.

The Montgomery Gymnasium was so far away from the main

campus when it was built in 1929 that the students had to give themselves extra time to get to their physical education classes. Each student was required to pass a swimming test in the forty-by-seventy-foot pool in the south wing. Tennis courts and playing fields had been laid out north of the dining hall, but the new gym made it possible to hold basketball games and even formal dances within the handsome Gothic-style structure.

In the late 1930s, federal funds became available for college buildings, and Rudolph Weaver designed a new dorm, Landis Hall, embellishing it with cast-stone medallions, plaques, and other decorative elements. He also drew up plans for a new infirmary, a new dining hall (the Johnston Building), and the Longmire Building, which was to be used as a student activity center.

President Conradi retired in 1941 and was succeeded by Dr. Doak Campbell, who would lead the school through the challenging years of World War II and the transition from a woman's college to a coeducational university. In 1945 the Tallahassee Branch of the University of Florida (TBUF) was organized to relieve pressure on the vastly crowded university, with student veterans living in barracks at Dale Mabry Field and taking classes at FSCW. By the time coeducation became official two years later, men were well established on the formerly all-female campus.

Florida State College for Women became Florida State University in May 1947, a transformation duly noted in the changed name on the iron arch over the entrance gates in front of Westcott. Cawthon Hall was the last of the Gothic-style buildings. Planned before the conversion but completed in 1948, it bears the letters FSCW, carved in decorative stone, in one of its west doorways.

After making do with makeshift housing, classroom, and office space during the 1940s, FSU exploded into an urgently needed building boom in the 1950s. Two eleven-story skyscraper dorms for men, Smith Hall and Kellum Hall, were built on land west of the main campus, and a new student center was completed in 1952. Although they might have some architectural references to the older buildings in the form of arcades, they made use of new building technologies and twentieth-century design trends. Doak Campbell

Stadium, used for commencement ceremonies as well as football games, was built in 1950 far to the west, anchoring what has become a large complex of playing fields and athletic facilities. The new Tully Gym didn't have air-conditioning, but the $1.7 million Music Building (the Kuersteiner Building) did, for the sake of the instruments.

The installation of two van de Graaff nuclear accelerators at FSU emphasized future expansion into the sciences. Thanks to federal grants for research in physics and chemistry, new buildings were planned for what was called "Sputnik City," the FSU Science Center.

In 1958, the Strozier Library replaced the original library built in the 1920s, which then became the home of the Graduate School (Dodd Hall). With rapid growth in enrollment in the next decade came new demands for dorms and academic buildings as well as facilities for the athletic program. The size of the campus almost doubled and more than seventeen major buildings were completed in the 1960s.

A disastrous fire swept through the Westcott Building in the spring of 1969, and the building had to be evacuated. Because of limited funds, it took seven years to complete the multimillion-dollar restoration. The historical exterior of Westcott was preserved, but the radically modern design of the new Fine Arts Building on Tennessee Street shocked Tallahassee traditionalists when it opened in 1970. The Law School, east of the main campus but closer to the judicial buildings near the state capitol, was built in the 1970s, and the College of Education consolidated its far-flung departments in the Stone Building across from the Demonstration School. The School of Music expanded in the late seventies and several more academic buildings sprouted within the FSU Science Center.

Commitment to the future takes planning and as the 1980s and 1990s have progressed, FSU's building strategy has taken into account not only new building and space needs but the preservation of older buildings. Most of the historic buildings on campus have been renovated to accommodate new technology and to prepare them for the twenty-first century. The new University Center wrapping around Doak Campbell Stadium reflects a heightened interest in the Gothic architectural heritage of FSU with its red-brick and stone accents expressed in turrets and gables, arches and arcades. Also part of this heritage is the dynamic modernism of the buildings constructed after 1950 with their clean lines and functional design.

A major research university such as Florida State University will continue to evolve and no doubt still impress new students that it looks just as a university should look.

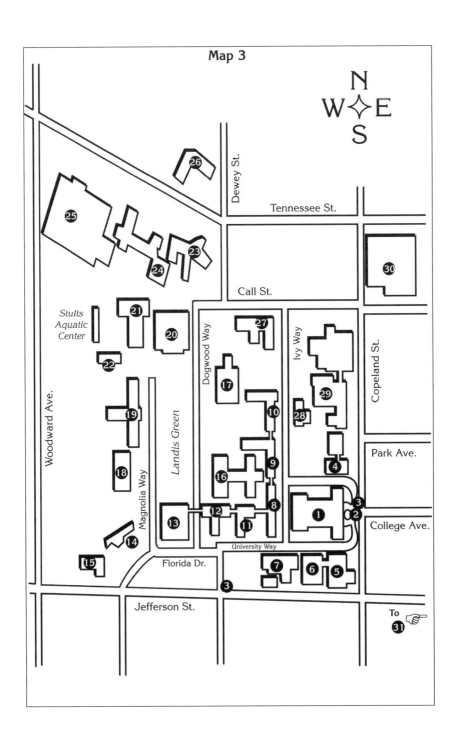

Map 3.
East Section of FSU Campus

1. Westcott Building
2. Westcott Fountain
3. Entrance Gates
4. Psychology Building
5. Diffenbaugh Building
6. Williams Building
7. Dodd Hall
8. Bryan Hall
9. Reynolds Hall
10. Jennie Murphree Hall
11. Broward Hall
12. Gilchrist Hall
13 Landis Hall
14. Deviney Hall
15. Dorman Hall
16. Johnston Building
17. Cawthon Hall
18. Shores Building
19. Montgomery Gymnasium
20. Strozier Library
21. Bellamy Building
22. Thagard Student Health Center
23. Conradi Biology Building
24. Rovetta Business Buildings
25. Oglesby Student Union
26. DeGraff Hall
27. Sandels Building
28. Longmire Building
29. Music Buildings
30. Fine Arts Building
31. College of Law (see map 1)

Westcott Building

Location: Copeland Street and College Avenue

The James D. Westcott Jr. Memorial Building was the second building designed by architect William Edwards for the FSCW campus. Completed in 1911, it was known simply as the Administration Building until the 1930s. It replaced College Hall, which had stood on the hill overlooking Tallahassee since 1855, when it was built for the West Florida Seminary. The dramatic facade of Westcott with its twin towers and battlements immediately made it a symbol for FSCW, and it continues to be the most photographed building on campus. The main entrance has elaborate stonework with reliefs of important dates in the school's history. Westcott originally housed the entire administrative function of the college, the library, classrooms, and an auditorium where

Westcott Building

students were once obliged to attend daily chapel services. The presence of unstable pipe clay, or Fuller's earth, beneath the building caused large cracks in the brick walls, a problem Westcott shared with the adjacent Education Building. In 1923 the north wing had to be rebuilt, and the auditorium was not back in service until 1926. In1936 the building was renamed for James D. Westcott Jr., a member of the state legislature and supreme court who had left a good portion of his estate to the school, which he had attended when it was Florida State College. In 1953 a grand new auditorium was completed and named for Miss Ruby Diamond, a beloved benefactor and a graduate of the Florida State College class of 1905, the last coed class until 1947 when FSCW became FSU. A fire in 1969 destroyed most of the building's interior but the reconstruction, which took more than six years to complete, preserved the original exterior. Administrative offices, including that of the president, are still located in Westcott. Look for the ornate pair of bronze memorial doors encased in glass near the entrance to the auditorium and, on the second floor, the bell that once called FSCW students to meals.

Westcott Fountain

Location: Copeland Street and College Avenue

This is a fountain for all seasons and all reasons: during severe winters icicles dripped from it; at times the water foamed and bubbled over when soap powder was added by pranksters; students have been tossed into it to celebrate or to cool off high spirits; coins are still pitched into it by wish makers; and thousands of graduates and their proud parents have been photographed in front of it. The white concrete fountain located in the circular court in front of Westcott is the focal point of the FSU entrance at the head of College Avenue. The central shaft of the fountain, which was recently rebuilt to the exact measurements of the original, is topped with a finial from which water cascades into two circular graduated basins and then into a sunken circular pool.

Westcott Fountain

The Westcott Fountain was donated by the classes of 1915 and 1917, which succeeded in their aim of creating a visual symbol and sense of tradition for FSCW. This contribution initiated the giving of class gifts, which has enriched FSCW and FSU in many ways throughout the years. A new fountain was recently erected across from Doak Campbell Stadium, a class gift commemorating the university's fiftieth anniversary, but the old fountain remains one of FSU's most treasured symbols.

Entrance Gates

Location: College Avenue and Jefferson Street

Framing the twin towers of Westcott and the fountain at the head of College Avenue is a stone-and-brick gateway of Gothic-revival styling, a gift of the classes of 1916 and 1918,

Gilchrist Entrance Gates

as noted by plaques in stone relief on each of the main piers. The lamp of learning was the symbol of the class of 1916, while a rose was emblematic of the women who graduated in 1918. The name on the ironwork that once read "Florida State College for Women" was changed in 1947 to "Florida State University." The medallion in the center of the arch bears the Florida state seal. A chain that once stretched between the main brick piers on Sundays and at night to indicate that the campus was closed to visitors was replaced in 1924 with iron gates to better protect the decorum and quiet of the campus at these times. The entrance has been widened to accommodate increased traffic, and the gates have been gone since 1964. On the south side of campus, opposite Gilchrist Hall and the Sweet Shop, is another set of gates, donated by the classes of 1933 and 1935, as shown in the medallion inset on the iron arch. Each of the main brick piers that flanks the entrance is connected to a smaller flanking pier by a rounded arch over the sidewalk.

Psychology Building–Francis Eppes Hall and Kellogg Building

Location: University Way, north of Westcott Building

I t is no surprise that in an era when Florida desperately needed a steady supply of teachers for its expanding public school system, the FSCW School of Education was viewed as an important asset. It was organized in 1910, with Nathaniel M. Salley serving as its dean until 1937. The first FSCW building devoted entirely to classroom use was completed in 1918 for the School of Education, situated in a prime location near the main entrance to the college. William Edwards designed the Tudor-style building. Interesting decorative details on its main facade include an owl, symbol of wisdom, and frogs perching on the low buttresses at the

Psychology Building

south entrance. In 1931 the walls of the building began to crack and the building was condemned. When it was rebuilt, much of the original material—red brick and stone trim—was reused, and dormers were added to provide more space in the attic. In the mid-1950s, the School of Education moved to a new building named for Dean Mode L. Stone. The original building was turned over to the psychology department, and the sign over the door was changed to read "Psychology" in large Gothic letters. In 1963, the adjoining Kellogg Psychology Research Building was completed. Although the style of this addition is modern, its scale and use of red brick with cast-concrete trim are in keeping with the older building to which it is connected by a bridge on each floor. It honors Winthrop N. Kellogg, who was acclaimed for his research with primates and dolphins. The Psychology Building, the oldest academic structure on campus, was renamed Francis Eppes Hall in 1997. Eppes, a grandson of Thomas Jefferson, was a Tallahassee civic leader in the nineteenth century. He had absorbed Jefferson's concepts regarding the importance of education and as mayor of Tallahassee in the 1840s, he offered the Florida legislature the land on which a local school stood as a site for the West Florida Seminary, the forerunner of FSU.

Diffenbaugh Building

Location: University Way, south of Westcott Building

T he Tudor arch at the north entrance to the Diffenbaugh Building is a remnant of the red-brick FSCW structure known as Science Hall, built on this site in 1922. Science Hall was located south of the Administration Building (Westcott), facing the Education Building (Psychology Building). Together these three structures formed a unified academic ensemble at the main entrance to the college. When the front section of the old Science Hall was demolished in the late 1970s, a few of its decorative features were incorporated into the new structure. The 1939

Diffenbaugh Building

addition to the building is still in place on the south side, with original windows, gable walls, and dormers. Professor of English Guy
Linton Diffenbaugh, for whom the building was named in 1964, was
appointed dean of the College of Arts and Sciences in 1943. He had
been on the faculty of FSCW since 1928 and also served as chair of
the English department for many years. Although the building originally housed the School of Home Economics, with classrooms and
laboratories for chemistry and physics, it became associated with the
humanities and is now the home of the College of Communication
and the modern language and linguistics departments.

Williams Building

Location: University Way

O riginally called the History Building when it was completed in 1927 (a plaque over one door bears the quotation, "History is a pageant not a philosophy"), the Williams Building has grown in stages, with additions that barely seemed to keep up with the growing need for classroom space on the FSCW campus. Architect Rudolph Weaver stamped the Tudor style on the red-brick building with its pointed arches and stone reliefs that echoed the prevailing campus style. The four-hundred-seat Augusta Conradi Theater, named in memory of President Conradi's wife, was added in 1931 and became the center for drama on campus. In 1963 the History Building was renamed to honor Professor Arthur Williams, who taught from 1903 (at the old coeducational Florida State College) to 1936. He was the first chairman of the history department and also served for twenty-four years as vice president of FSCW. The Williams Building is undergoing extensive renovation.

Williams Building

Dodd Hall

Dodd Hall

Location: University and Ivy Ways

T he gold-leaf message above the entrance to Dodd Hall proclaims, "The half of knowledge is to know where to find knowledge," a most suitable inscription for the school's first library. President Conradi had pleaded with the Board of Control for a library for years, but the west wing was not completed until 1924. It was designed by William Edwards, who was responsible for setting the Tudor-Gothic tone of the early buildings on campus. The 1928 addition was designed by his successor, Rudolph Weaver. The elaborate detailing of the splendid main entrance includes bold, colorful terra-cotta insignia and moldings around the doorway, windows with Gothic tracery, and the shining Gothic lettering of the anonymous maxim. Louise Richardson was director of the library from 1922 until 1956. She supervised the construction of both wings and started the library science program at FSCW. The elaborately patterned plaster ceiling and decorative frieze in the lobby add a note of grandeur to the interior. The Werkmeister Humanities Reading Room west of the entrance has a lofty, open-beamed ceiling and seven paired windows set in recessed arches on each side. A stained-glass window at the west end, created in the 1970s by Bob and Joanne Bishoff, depicts a colorful collage of four favorite FSU buildings. In 1961, after the new Strozier Library opened, the building was renamed to honor William G. Dodd, a professor of English and dean of the College of Arts and Sciences from 1910 to 1944. Hired by Dr. Conradi in 1910, Dodd was a great favorite of the students and helped shape the academic direction of the institution. At various times Dodd Hall has housed the offices of WFSU-TV, the dean of the College of Arts and Sciences, the Graduate School, and the Mildred and Claude Pepper Library. It is currently the home of the departments of philosophy, classics, religion, and American and Florida studies. A recent addition in the rear houses a large auditorium.

Bryan Hall

Location: Ivy Way

B ryan Hall might be the setting for a romantic Gothic novel, with its crenelated parapet and twin dark towers marking the entrance. As the oldest building on the FSU campus, built in 1907, the fortresslike structure has a well-deserved reputation for endurance. What was once a swampy hollow in front of the red-brick building was turned into a sunken garden in 1909, one of the first landscaping improvements on campus. A bronze shield on the triple-arcaded, recessed front porch is a tribute to William James Bryan, a native of Florida and a U.S. senator, for whom the building was named. He had recently died of typhoid and the building became his memorial. Bryan Hall, primarily a dormitory, was also the social center of the campus. The atrium, Bryan's main lobby, was the scene of receptions and tea parties and a place where students

Bryan Hall

could entertain their friends, families, and dates. Many student groups held their meetings in Bryan Hall lounges. Stairways once led up to the towers, where the Chi Omega and Kappa Delta sororities met when they were first organized. When the roof of the venerable building collapsed in the 1940s, major renovations were made and the towers became inaccessible. Used for administrative purposes for years after a disastrous fire in 1969 put Westcott out of commission, Bryan Hall is once more a residence for first-year students. It became the first Learning Community, modeled on English universities, where students take classes and live under the same roof.

Reynolds Hall

Location: Ivy Way

Reynolds Hall, completed in 1913, was the second dormitory designed by William Edwards for FSCW. Instead of continuing the crenelated roofline of Bryan Hall, he introduced gabled tile roofs with decks and gabled pavilions. The west section of

Reynolds Hall

the L-shaped building was extended in 1920. Reynolds Hall is connected to Bryan and Jennie Murphree with arcades and was originally also linked by an arcade to the infirmary. The residence hall was named for Mrs. Mary Reynolds, the first Lady Principal and supervisor of dormitories, a motherly woman who served as surrogate parent for young FSCW students away from home for the first time. The recently renovated residence hall accommodates 243 students in furnished suites, each wired for computers—indispensable tools for today's scholars. Without leaving their dorm, residents of Reynolds Hall can do their laundry, whip up a meal in one of the kitchens, gather with friends to watch a game in the TV lounge, or attend a social function in the formal lounge.

Jennie Murphree Hall

Location: Ivy Way

Completed in 1922, the residence hall honors Jennie Henderson Murphree, the wife of Albert A. Murphree, who was president of the college from 1905 to 1909. Mrs. Murphree, a Tallahassee girl, graduated from Florida State College, FSCW's predecessor, in 1905. Dr. Murphree, who assumed the presidency of the University of Florida in Gainesville in 1909, laid the groundwork for a strong liberal arts curriculum that eventually made FSCW one of the most respected women's colleges in the South. The fourth red-brick dormitory constructed to accommodate a growing student population was designed by William Edwards. The architect continued the Tudor architectural tradition he had begun in 1907 with Bryan Hall. Jennie Murphree Hall has a gabled, red-tile roof, an oriel window on the east side, and stone reliefs at the doorways, some of them with elaborate and whimsical designs. Over the northeast entrance is a crest with three flaming torches, the legend "Vires, Artes, Mores" (strength, skill, customs), and the words "Femina Perfecta" (the complete woman). Like the other residence halls built before 1940, Jennie Murphree Hall is connected to its

Jennie Murphree Hall

neighboring dormitory, Reynolds, by an arcade, and like the other older dorms it has frequently been remodeled. Over the years, single rooms have given way to suites, air-conditioning has been added, and rooms have been wired for phones and computers. An all-female residence hall, Jennie is the home of a community living program for students majoring in engineering, mathematics, and science.

Broward Hall

Broward Hall

Location: Florida Drive

The recently renovated Broward Hall was the third brick residence hall built for FSCW students. Constructed in 1917, eight years after Bryan Hall was completed, it helped alleviate a pressing need for dormitory space. The three-story, L-shaped building was designed by William Edwards, the architect who designed all campus buildings between 1907 and 1924. The first women to inhabit the dorm in the fall of 1918 found no doors, no lights, and no beds, due to the rush to move students into the residence hall. At first it also lacked parlors (most important for meeting with visiting families or gentlemen callers). With its crenelated parapet surrounding the flat roof it seems a natural extension of Bryan Hall, but at first it was not even connected to Bryan; an arcade was added when Broward's west wing was completed between 1921 and 1922. It was refurbished in the 1930s and the Broward Club Room was set aside for the use of student organizations. Additional arcades connected Broward to Gilchrist and Landis Halls when they were built, allowing students to walk through all six dorms without going outside. Broward Hall was named for Napoleon Bonaparte Broward, governor of the state in 1905, the year Florida Female College was founded. The Jacksonville native, a successful businessman and political leader, was elected in 1904 and served until 1909.

Gilchrist Hall

Location: Florida Drive

This newly renovated dormitory was built between 1926 and 1928. The T-shaped structure with gabled terra-cotta roof and brick walls, designed by Board of Control architect Rudolph Weaver, follows the collegiate-Gothic or Tudor style of the earlier buildings. The outer side of each section has a cast-stone arched entry, and bay windows add to the interest of the south wing. When it opened, Gilchrist Hall had modern amenities such as two lights and electrical outlets in each room and cozy parlors for entertaining. The residents were also delighted with the main lounge, which had an intricately carved fireplace and doorway moldings

Gilchrist Hall

with a graceful grapevine motif. Gilchrist was connected to Broward Hall, and in 1939, when Landis Hall was completed, a three-story arcade linked it to Gilchrist. This residence hall was named for Governor Albert W. Gilchrist, a staunch friend of FSCW. During his term as governor from 1909 to 1913, he took an active interest in the school and left a bequest to provide scholarships for students in need. Gilchrist Hall is home to 229 students who occupy freshly refurbished single and double rooms, now wired to accommodate computers and cable TV.

Landis Hall

Location: between Florida Drive and Landis Green

For years the largest dormitory on the FSCW campus was Landis Hall, completed as a federally funded Public Works Administration project in 1939. Although the Great

Landis Hall

Landis Green

Depression was a time of hardship and economic stress for the nation and the state, the federal government's willingness to help educational institutions find the money to build facilities, thereby providing construction jobs for unemployed workers, was a great boon to the college. The new residence hall was long overdue and the 370 students who moved into it in 1939 appreciated its up-to-date appointments such as a house phone in every room, elevators, and recreation rooms and lounges. The sundeck on the roof was popular too, and in the 1940s aviators from nearby Dale Mabry Field often flew low to inspect the topless sunbathers. The five-story red-brick building was designed by Rudolph Weaver in the prevailing Tudor style. It is one of the most elaborate buildings on campus, with bay windows on the side wings, an oriel window above the south entrance, and stone ornamentation such as the three plaques depicting women in their life roles: one holding a gavel, one reading a book, and one with a baby. On the south side of Landis Hall a large open courtyard, partly filled by a sandy volleyball court, is enclosed by a brick colonnade that links the two side wings. The north entrance faces Landis Green, an open, park-like quadrangle in the center of the older part of the campus and a favorite place for sunbathing, outdoor classes, and relaxing on sunny days. The dormitory was named for Judge Cary D. Landis, a former state attorney general who was a strong supporter of FSCW and higher education in general. Landis Hall, which now houses more than four hundred students, is the home of the Honors and Scholars Program for highly motivated students. The single, double, triple, and quad rooms are all wired for computers and serious studying is expected of the residents.

Deviney Hall

Location: Florida Drive

F lorida Hall, the first high-rise, modern residence for women, opened on the FSU campus in 1952. The eight-story brick building with horizontal bands of concrete window awnings was a major departure from the traditional Tudor styling of the other women's dorms. Today the air-conditioned residence hall houses 245 men and women students in single, double, or triple rooms, each wired for computer use. Other amenities are kitchens and laundry rooms, a recreation room and sundeck, and a spacious patio on the north side. The building honors Professor Ezda May Deviney, who taught zoology for thirty-three years. After earning her Ph.D. from the University of North Carolina, she joined the FSCW faculty in 1924 and was chair of the FSU Department of Zoology until her death in 1964. Florida Hall was renamed for Dr. Deviney in 1965.

Deviney Hall

Dorman Hall

Location: Jefferson Street

D
r. Olivia Nelson Dorman was a distinguished professor of classics. She was popular with FSCW students and helped them organize some college traditions such as Torch Night, an event during which members of the sophomore class welcomed freshman women. She was appointed dean of students in 1934 and wisely revised some of the outmoded social codes regarding dating and dancing. Dr. Dorman returned to the classroom when the college became coed, but not before helping with the transition of student government when male students joined the women on the FSU campus in 1947. Completed and dedicated in 1959, a year after her death, this modern and functional residence hall for women rose a full eight stories on the west edge of the campus, surrounded by tall pine trees. At that time students were expected

Dorman Hall

to stay in their rooms to study during "quiet hours" (between 7:30 and 10:00 P.M.), and room inspections were held to make sure students kept their rooms clean and tidy. Today 276 women students live in the double dormitory rooms, refurbished and refitted to accommodate computers and cable TV.

Johnston Building

Location: Dogwood Way

The Suwannee Dining Hall, completed in 1913, was designed in the collegiate-Gothic or Tudor style, and an addition to the north end in 1922 provided more space in the one huge room where all students and faculty took their meals. In 1938 the Seminole Dining Hall, with its lofty beamed ceiling and

Johnston Building

arched windows like those in the refectories at Oxford University, was added to accommodate the growing number of students. Rudolph Weaver redesigned the building so that its main entrance faced west, the first building to be oriented toward the direction of future campus expansion. The exterior of the monumental building resembles Dodd Hall, with shouldered buttresses spaced between each window bay. The two-story entrance has a molded stone arch with pierced tracery, and a noble sculpture of a woman presides just below the apex of the arch. After 1947, when FSCW became a coed university, the communal dining style with linen tablecloths, engraved silverware, and fresh flowers on the tables changed to cafeteria style. The Seminole Dining Hall became Johnston Hall in 1984 to honor William H. Johnston, a Jacksonville hotel owner who was a major benefactor of the university. He gave the FSU Foundation the Duval Hotel in Jacksonville, one of the first major private gifts of the 1970s. When the building was no longer used as the main campus dining facility, the interior space was converted to office space and classrooms.

Cawthon Hall

Location: Dogwood Way

C awthon was one of the last buildings on campus to conform to the Tudor or Gothic style. Guy C. Fulton, architect for the Board of Control in 1946 when the plans were drawn up, respected the style used in earlier buildings designed by William Edwards and Rudolph Weaver. Even though the dormitory was not completed until 1948, after the school had become Florida State University, a stone relief at the west entry features the letters FSCW in one corner, with a floral design twining around the decorative lettering. The building's many dormers, gables, and bay windows, in addition to its stone trim, contribute to its traditional styling, and the hollow-square plan provides a protected inner courtyard. Cawthon serves as headquarters for the FSU Housing Office and provides living accommodations for 268 transfer students. The residence hall was named for Sarah Landrum Cawthon, who was appointed first dean of the College Home in 1910, a position that later became dean of student affairs. "Tissie," as she was called, served as surrogate mother and set strict regulations of social conduct for students. Cawthon Hall is said to be haunted by Tissie's ghost, a friendly spirit clad in a green dress.

Cawthon Hall

Shores Building

Location: Magnolia Way

D r. Louis Shores joined the faculty of FSCW in 1946, just a year before it became FSU. He established the School of Library Science, originally housed in Strozier Library. It is now called the School of Information Studies, indicating the broader mission of the school and the scope of professional positions its graduates are prepared to fill. The handsome new facility for the school was built between 1980 and 1981 on the west side of Landis Green. Within the three-story brick building are classrooms and offices and a separate library facility, the Harold Goldstein Library (named for the second dean of the school), which supports the research of the school.

Shores Building

Montgomery Gymnasium

Location: Magnolia Way

T he Montgomery Gymnasium, the first athletic facility built on campus, complemented the other Tudor-style buildings on campus. Crenelated parapets repeat an exterior design found on Bryan and Gilchrist Halls, and the oriel window over the arched entrance is a mark of the collegiate-Gothic style that was popular at older colleges and universities. The gym opened in 1929 and the large tiled swimming pool became familiar to each student, as one of the requirements for graduation was demonstrated proficiency in swimming. Fierce basketball and volleyball competitions between class teams and later, other schools, were held in the main gym, whose gallery could seat four hundred spectators. It also doubled as a setting for dance classes and occasionally formal dances. Stylized relief symbols of bowling and badminton embellish doorways on the north wing, completed in 1949. The Montgomery

Montgomery Gymnasium

Detail of Montgomery Gymnasium

Gym pool was the home of the famous Tarpon Club. Formed in 1937 by the school's lifesaving crew, the synchronized swimming team was featured in a 1939 movie short filmed at Wakulla Springs by sportscaster Grantland Rice. Renowned for their theatrical effects and stunning routines, members of the Tarpon Club thrilled audiences with water ballet shows. The Nancy Smith Fichter Dance Theater is also located in the gym, a reminder of the importance of dance in FSCW's physical education programs. Katherine Montgomery, for whom the gym was named, graduated from FSCW in 1918 and became its director of physical education in 1923. She developed the school's athletic programs and taught most of the PE classes for years. "Miss Katy" encouraged healthy exercise and intramural sports, even devising activities for less athletically gifted students. When FSCW became FSU in 1947, men and women lined up together for the first time to register for classes in the Montgomery Gym, the largest available space on campus for this recurring ritual.

Strozier Library

Location: Dogwood Way, facing Landis Green

The FSU library devoted to the humanities and social sciences was named for Dr. Robert Manning Strozier, president of FSU from 1957 to 1960. President Strozier was well liked and respected, and during his time in office the university and its academic and athletic programs expanded rapidly. After his untimely death the main library, completed in 1956, was named in his honor. An annex completed in 1967 added additional space for the library collection, which has grown to encompass more than two million books and periodicals. The contemporary style of the Strozier Library continued the traditional campus look of brick and stone, and the three-story entrance facade with its broad terrace and columns facing Landis Green is imposing and dignified. One of six libraries on the main campus, Strozier is equipped with more than

Strozier Library

two hundred computer terminals for the increasingly important task of electronic information searches. However, ancient volumes, first editions, rare books, and author's manuscripts are available for study and research in the Special Collections area.

Bellamy Building

Location: west of the Strozier Library

D
r. Raymond F. Bellamy, for whom the building was named, organized the sociology department at FSCW in 1918 and served as its chair until 1956. Known for his sense of humor, Bellamy must have enjoyed the outcome of the controversy that erupted in the 1920s when local churchmen attacked him for the content of his sociology textbooks with their references to evolu-

tion and Freud. The offending books were removed, making them even more interesting to the students, who found copies of Freud's books and shared them with their curious friends. The modern building named for the amiable Dr. Bellamy was completed in1967 as the home of a number of social sciences departments. With more than one hundred thousand square feet and more than four hundred rooms, it was the largest academic classroom building on campus. Windows disappear in the geometric pattern of the outer walls, with the architectural emphasis on crisp horizontal and vertical lines. The south wing is three stories high, and the north wing rises seven stories. Look for the offices of the departments of anthropology, Asian studies, criminology, economics, geography, history, political science, public administration, sociology, and women's studies in the Bellamy Building.

Bellamy Building

Thagard Student Health Center

Location: north of Montgomery Gym

Florida native and NASA astronaut Norman E. Thagard received his bachelor's and master's degrees in engineering sciences from FSU in the mid-1960s and went on to become a medical doctor in 1977. The following year he was accepted for astronaut training, which led to a six-day mission on board the Challenger space shuttle in 1983. Thagard honored his alma mater by lofting FSU memorabilia into space with him, and Mission Control played the "FSU Fight Song" to wake up the crew on their reentry day. Thagard, who delivered the December 1985 commencement address, was honored in 1986 when FSU named the Student Health Center for him. In 1995 the FSU astronaut-alum spent six more weeks in space as the first American astronaut on the Russian

Thagard Student Health Center

MIR spacecraft. The Thagard Student Health Center replaced the original infirmary building located west of the old dorms, which is now the Regional Rehabilitation Building. The modern medical facility, located near the Montgomery Gym and the Stults Aquatic Center, has a variety of outpatient clinics that specialize in such areas as dentistry, gynecology, allergy treatment, and minor surgery. Students can also get immunization shots here, have prescriptions filled, and get advice on good nutrition.

Conradi Biology Building

Location: Dewey and Call Streets

D r. Edward Conradi was the second president of FSCW, succeeding A. A. Murphree in 1909 and serving until his retirement in 1941. A native of Ohio, Conradi had a forceful personality and was an able administrator. He was responsible

Conradi Biology Building

for having Clinton Avenue renamed College Avenue and getting the street paved to the entrance gates. Conradi led the college through the trying years of World War I and the Great Depression, building a prominent and respected institution that was referred to as the "Vassar of the South." The modern brick building named for him was completed in 1956 in a modified L shape, with three floors of classrooms and laboratories devoted to the biological sciences. The DNA Sequencing Facility is housed in the Conradi Building, and the greenhouses set on the adjacent grounds are used for biology research by students and faculty.

Rovetta Business Buildings

Location: east of Oglesby Student Union

The FSU College of Business occupies two connected buildings, one built in 1952 and the other constructed in 1982. Both represent the architectural spirit and building tech-

Newer section of the Rovetta Business Buildings

nology of their times and offer an interesting contrast in their well-landscaped setting. The man for whom they were named, Dean Charles Rovetta, was a professor of accounting and served as dean of the college from 1953 to 1973. One of the largest divisions at FSU, the College of Business enrolls undergraduates and graduates in seven departments: accounting, finance, hospitality administration, information and management sciences, management, marketing, and risk management.

Older section of the Rovetta Business Buildings

Oglesby Student Union

Location: Woodward Avenue

In the 1950s a new student center with post office, snack bar, and jukebox was built on the west side of the campus, replacing the Longmire Building as a campus gathering place. It has since been enlarged time and again, expanding to accommodate more and more students and more and more features. In 1973 it was named

Oglesby Student Union

for Dean Roscoe R. Oglesby. One of the chief planners of the new student union, he believed that all university life should be a learning experience for students, not only what they absorb in the classroom. A professor of government and a scholar of international law, Oglesby served as dean of students from 1954 to 1964, during a period of incredible growth for FSU. Today students can do their banking here, have their hair cut, buy concert tickets, get their bikes repaired, see a movie, listen to live music, eat lunch, pick out a greeting card, take a painting class, or relax in one of the comfortable lounges. The Oglesby Art Gallery mounts juried shows and displays the works of groups and individual artists. For a hands-on approach, the Oglesby Art Center is open for leisure classes in a wide range of arts and crafts. More than two hundred clubs and organizations, from accounting and aikido to wrestling and water skiing, meet at the Oglesby Student Union, which is also the home of the Student Government Organization.

DeGraff Hall

Location: Tennessee and Dewey Streets

The residence hall located across Tennessee Street from the Conradi Building is home to 140 men and women students and the innovative Cultural Awareness Program that emphasizes multicultural education. Each of the single or double rooms is wired for computers and fully furnished, as are most FSU dorm accommodations. The modern, V-shaped building opened in 1950 as a men's residence hall. It was dedicated in 1961 to Dr. Mark H. DeGraff, a popular professor in the College of Education who was also director of the Test Service Bureau until his retirement in 1957. The brick dormitory with large oak trees on its front lawn is accessible to the main FSU campus via a tunnel that passes beneath Tennessee Street.

DeGraff Hall

Sandels Building

Location: Ivy Way and Call Street

D ean Margaret Sandels, head of the School of Home Economics from 1922 to 1958, was successful in building the school's enrollment from 48 students when she launched the program to 366 majors at her retirement. It is now called the College of Human Sciences and concentrates on research and teaching in the areas of nutrition and exercise, clothing and housing, and family and child services. The functional, F-shaped building was constructed in 1956 and has undergone extensive renovation recently, including a new east facade that blends with the Gothic architectural tradition of the adjacent older residence halls.

Sandels Building

Longmire Building

Location: Ivy Way

U ntil the Rowena Longmire Student–Alumnae Union opened in 1938, there was no place on campus set aside solely for social functions and campus organizations. Because loyal alumnae had contributed generously to funding the building, it also served as headquarters of the FSCW Alumnae Association. Rudolph Weaver designed the five-story building, which was placed at the center of campus facing a row of dormitories. Although it lacks some of the heavier Gothic features such as buttresses and crenelation, the Longmire Building is very much in the style of the earlier buildings; it is simply a more streamlined version. The building was named for Rowena Longmire, who came to teach English in 1906 and remained on the faculty for thirty-two years. She received FSCW's first honorary degree in 1912, a master of arts. Miss Longmire was vitally interested in the lives of the students, and it was through her efforts that the Alumnae Association was founded. She served as the first president of the organization. Initially a game room, a soda shop, and the offices of the college newspaper, the *Flambeau*, were located in the ground-level space. A large lounge and social areas filled the main floor, noted for its handsome woodwork, and offices were on the floor above. A few guest bedrooms were available on the fourth floor for visiting alumnae, while storage space and meeting rooms for clubs occupied the top floor. When the FSU College of Law was organized in 1966, the Longmire Building was its home until permanent quarters in B. K. Roberts Hall were available.

Longmire Building

Kuersteiner and Housewright Music Buildings

Location: Copeland and Call Streets

The School of Music is widely recognized for its excellence and its distinguished faculty. The Kuersteiner Music Building, named for the second dean of the school, was completed in 1948 and reflects in its design the transition from Gothic styling to a contemporary architectural look. Architect Guy

Kuersteiner Music Building

Fulton used the older style on the eastern section but incorporated a one-thousand-seat modern amphitheater with square columns supporting a curved colonnade. The building was the first in Tallahassee to have air-conditioning, a feature included chiefly to protect the musical instruments but most appreciated by students and faculty as well. The Opperman Music Hall honors Ella Scoble Opperman, who directed the FSCW School of Music from 1911 to 1944. It was dedicated to her in 1952 at a concert performed by the University Symphony and conducted by Ernst von Dohnanyi, the acclaimed Hungarian composer, conductor, and pianist who had joined the FSU faculty in 1949. A new music building, named for the third dean of the college, Wiley Housewright, was completed in 1979. Although very modern and functional in appearance, it has elements that respect the early architectural tradition of the campus. It is of red brick with cast-concrete trim and is connected to the older music building by an open bridge that suggests the arcades used throughout the historic campus. The Housewright Building contains the Allen Music Library and the Dohnanyi Recital Hall. In addition to the FSU Marching Chiefs, who perform at football games, professional solo performers and ensembles of musicians, from opera choruses and glee clubs to jazz bands and chamber music quartets, perform more than three hundred recitals and concerts throughout the year for students and the general public. Augmenting the four performance spaces in the School of Music is the fifteen-hundred-seat Ruby Diamond Auditorium in Westcott, the venue for opera performances and major concerts.

Fine Arts Building

Location: Tennessee and Copeland Streets

The bold interaction of rounded and flat surfaces that distinguishes the dark-brick Fine Arts Building was considered a radical departure from the more traditional architecture of the campus when it opened in 1970 with a gala Fine Arts Festival.

Fine Arts Building

Stars of stage and screen like Tony Randall and Claire Bloom were seen strolling around the campus, and Gian Carlo Menotti staged a new play in the five-hundred-seat MainStage auditorium. To continue the benefits students derive from working with seasoned professionals, each year well-known actors and dancers spend time mentoring those enrolled in the School of Theatre and the School of Visual Arts and Dance. FSU's professional fine arts training program is ranked among the top ten in the nation. The university is also the home of the Charles MacArthur Center for the American Theatre, founded in 1972 in honor of the husband of actress Helen Hayes. Also in the Fine Arts Building is the Museum of Fine Arts, which features exhibits ranging from the hyper-realistic sculptures of Duane Hanson and audacious women artists to displays of ethnic art and works from FSU's permanent collection numbering more than three thousand. FSU provides a notable cultural asset to students and the general public—an exciting spectrum of the visual and performing arts at this center located on the north edge of the campus, close to the FSU music buildings with their world-renowned offerings of opera, jazz, symphonic, and new world music.

College of Law

Location: Jefferson Street and Martin Luther King Jr. Boulevard

T he 116 charter members of the FSU Law School met in 1966 in the Longmire Building. In 1973 the new law school moved to its permanent quarters, located east of the main campus but close to the state and federal court buildings in downtown Tallahassee. Former Florida Supreme Court Chief Justice B. K. Roberts, for whom the main building of the College of Law was named, was instrumental in securing funds for the law library, which was first set up in the basement of the Longmire Building where the soda shop was once located. The new library building, adjacent to the Roberts Hall, was dedicated in 1985. In contrast to the severe, modern styling of these two buildings is the adjacent Village Green to the east. Initiated in the 1980s by Law School Dean Talbot "Sandy" D'Alemberte, now president of FSU, this ensemble of

College of Law , Village Green

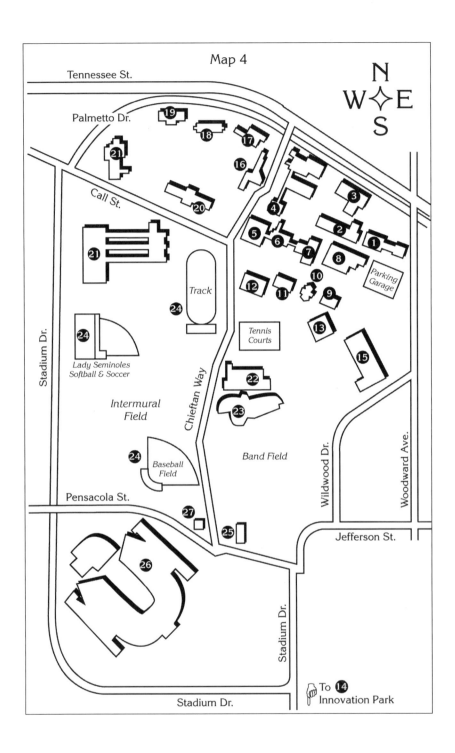

Map 4

Tennessee St.

Palmetto Dr.

Call St.

Stadium Dr.

Track

Tennis
Courts

Parking
Garage

Lady Seminoles
Softball & Soccer

Intermural
Field

Chieftan Way

Band Field

Baseball
Field

Wildwood Dr.

Woodward Ave.

Pensacola St.

Jefferson St.

Stadium Dr.

To ⓮
Innovation Park

Stadium Dr.

Map 4.
West Section of FSU Campus

1. Carraway Building
2. Carothers Hall
3. Love Building
4. Keen Physics Research Building
5. Biology Building
6. Molecular Biophysics Building
7. Dittmer Chemistry Laboratory
8. Dirac Science Library
9. Oceanography and Statistics Building
10. Fisher Lecture Hall
11. Hoffman Teaching Laboratory
12. Biomedical Research Facility
13. Nursing Building
14. FAMU/FSU School of Engineering (see map 2)
15. Mendenhall Maintenance Complex
16. Smith Hall
17. Kellum Hall
18. Rogers Hall
19. McCollum Hall
20. Salley Hall
21. Stone Building and FSU School
22. Tully Gym
23. Leach Student Recreation Center
24 Other Athletic Facilities
25. Haskins Circus Complex
26. Doak Campbell Stadium and University Center
27. Heritage Tower

buildings was designed to re-create the intimate ambiance of London's Inns of Court and is modeled after buildings designed by Thomas Jefferson for the University of Virginia. The Rotunda provides a gracious assembly place for law students, faculty, lawyers, and judges, and four nineteenth-century wood frame buildings, moved to this site and restored, are linked to it by walkways and a colonnade enclosing the Green.

Carraway Building

Location: Woodward Avenue

The Carraway Building, completed in 1953, was renamed in 1965 for Senator Franklin Wilson Carraway, a legislator long associated with the development of Florida State

Carraway Building

University. The native of Tallahassee was the president of the local Coca-Cola Bottling Company and served on the boards of several area banks. Carraway was active in public service, serving for five years in the Florida House of Representatives and for five terms in the Florida Senate. He presided over the state senate in 1963. The Department of Geology, which celebrated its fiftieth anniversary in 1998, is housed in the building, which was partly funded by the National Science Foundation. The earth sciences, particularly environmental geology, paleontology, and hydrogeology, are the focus of research undertaken in the laboratories, classrooms, and faculty offices within the structure. Interesting displays of minerals, fossils, and shells line the halls, and the Antarctic Marine Geology Core Library, the largest collection of drill-core material from the ocean floor of the Antarctic, is housed here.

Carothers Hall

Location: Woodward Avenue and Palmetto Drive

Carothers Hall

A small but graceful modern portico with curving lines marks the north entrance to the building. Metal-and-glass window walls give the four-story brick structure a strong horizontal image. A large computer lab on the third floor draws many students to the building at all hours, while offices and classrooms for a number of departments occupy the other floors. Milton Carothers, for whom the building was named, was appointed registrar of FSCW in 1943. In 1946, when more than five hundred men enrolled in the Tallahassee Branch of the University of Florida (TBUF) and settled in to live at the former Dale Mabry Field, or West Campus, Carothers was appointed dean of TBUF. When FSCW became FSU, he became first dean of the Graduate School and served as acting president after the death of President Strozier in 1960.

Love Building

Location: Palmetto Drive

Love Building

Offices, classrooms, and laboratories for the computer science, mathematics, and meteorology departments are located in this modern brick building, completed in 1961. The entrance lobby features slate-covered walls, and colored tiles and windows set with glass bricks brighten the broad stairwells. A small observatory is on the roof of the five-story building. It was first called the Mathematics and Meteorology Building but was renamed in 1964 for James Jay Love, the former mayor of Quincy and a prominent civic leader. The Gadsden County businessman, banker, and planter served as president of the Board of Control and was instrumental in securing funding for the space-age science and technology building. A plaque in the lobby states, "He gave devoted, unselfish service to his community, his state, and his country."

Keen Physics Research Building

Location: Chieftain Way

The Keen Building, completed in 1965, rises gracefully from a broad plaza, its flat roof lightly supported by rows of cast-concrete columns on three sides. A balconied pavilion forms the top floor. Partly funded by a large federal research grant, the building became the home of the Geophysical Fluid Dynamics Institute, an internationally recognized program that brings together scientists from a wide variety of fields to collaborate on research in the earth and space sciences. The MARTECH center, concentrating on materials research and technology, is also located in the seven-story building. The windowless research core with its pre-cast exterior panels was built to specifications of the most up-to-date technology of the time. The building was dedicated in 1966 and named for James Velma Keen, a Tallahassee attorney who served as chair of the Florida Nuclear Development Commission from 1955 to 1961. He was a major influence in persuading the 1957 Florida legislature to appropriate funds for facilities for an expanded program of nuclear research. A plaque in the lobby notes his contributions: "His name may be forgotten but it will never be lost for it is woven into the stuff of other men's lives." A covered arcade connects the Keen Building to the Harold F. Richards Undergraduate Physics Building, completed in 1977 and named for a professor of physics who taught at FSCW for twenty-seven years, and to the Nuclear Research Building.

Keen Physics Research Building

Biology Building

Location: Chieftain Way

C lassrooms, offices, and laboratories devoted to the biological sciences are located in this large brick building, one of several on campus where teaching and research in the life processes of plant and animal species are concentrated. It is linked to the adjacent Molecular Biophysics Building.

Molecular Biophysics Building

Location: south of the Keen Building

W hen the former meadows and pastures of West Campus began to sprout multistoried buildings in the new FSU Science Center in the 1950s and 1960s, the field of molecular biophysics was the focus of one of the new struc-

Molecular Biophysics Building

tures. Space-age research offered great promise and advanced laboratory facilities were installed, including those that support the work of the Institute of Molecular Biophysics. The imposing mass of the red-brick building is marked by narrow vertical bands of windows. Footbridges, some of them glass enclosed, provide access to adjacent structures and to the broad plaza that forms a central open space in the FSU Science Center.

Dittmer Chemistry Laboratory

Location: south of the Keen Building

The Chemistry Unit I Building was renamed and dedicated in 1979 in honor of Karl Dittmer, who chaired the FSU Department of Chemistry from 1949 until 1958. He was

Dittmer Chemistry Laboratory

instrumental in organizing the graduate program in chemistry and in 1964 was appointed vice president for academic affairs. This eight-story building with its massive vertical buttresses was one of the largest buildings in the FSU Science Center. Classrooms and laboratories to support the teaching and research activities of the divisions of analytical, inorganic, organic, and physical chemistry, as well as biochemistry, were placed within its fortresslike walls.

Dirac Science Library

Location: south of Carothers Building

T he FSU science library completed in 1988 was named for English physicist Paul A. M. Dirac, the 1933 Nobel Prize winner who spent the last fourteen years of his life on the FSU physics faculty. Dr. Dirac received the prestigious award for his

Dirac Science Library

relative wave equation, developed in 1927. He arrived at FSU in 1969 after retiring as Lucasian Professor of Mathematics at Cambridge University, a position first held by Sir Isaac Newton. A statue of the Nobel laureate has been placed on the lawn next to the library, shaded by oak and pine trees. Bands of dark-glass window walls alternate with panels of red brick, and the dramatic entrance leads to a spacious interior. A central feature is the columnar stairwell that rises from the main floor. The first three stories of the building house more than five hundred thousand volumes related to the sciences, as well as periodicals and journals. The fourth floor is occupied by the Supercomputer Computation Research Institute, a facility used by scientists from many disciplines who utilize the high-performance computers to investigate a wide spectrum of theoretical and experimental concepts.

Oceanography and Statistics Building

Location: Call Street

A central pavilion lends emphasis to the symmetrical facade of the three-story modern building that is the home of the oceanography and statistics departments. The research orientation of the oceanography department is supported in classrooms and laboratories in the building where faculty and students explore the mysteries of the sea. A multidisciplinary approach is the key to understanding the physical properties of the world's oceans and the diversity of animal and plant life found there. Students learning about the biological, chemical, geological, and other aspects of oceanography also receive hands-on experience in the FSU marine laboratory located on the Gulf of Mexico as well as in those on campus. Computer labs in the building are in high demand for modeling problems and solutions in both departments.

Oceanography and Statistics Building

Fisher Lecture Hall

Location: south of the Dirac Library

C onveniently located in the heart of the FSU Science Center, this small building with its configuration of steeply slanted walls encompasses two large lecture halls. It was named for Dr. James Robert Fisher, who served on the faculty of the chemistry department from 1955 to 1976. Fisher was honored as a biochemist, teacher, scholar, and humanist at the dedication of the building in 1978.

Fisher Lecture Hall

Hoffman Teaching Laboratory of Chemistry

Location: west of the Fisher Lecture Hall

Katherine Blood Hoffman was a 1936 graduate of FSCW. During the hard times of the Great Depression, "Kitty" Blood paid for her sophomore year with several truckloads of oranges from her father's grove in Winter Haven, held a "dining-room scholarship" the next year, and received a Gilchrist Scholarship in her senior year. After graduating from FSCW with a bachelor of science degree in bacteriology and from Columbia University with a master of arts degree, she returned to her alma mater in 1940 to teach chemistry and became a full professor in 1973, teaching thousands of students in her forty-two-year career. She served for several years in

Hoffman Teaching Laboratory of Chemistry

the 1960s as FSU's dean of women and was the first woman president of the Faculty Senate. In 1985 the Katherine B. Hoffman Teaching Laboratory of Chemistry was named for her. The imposing building features horizontal bands of gray concrete on a brick-grill background and windowless vertical towers, reflecting the modern trends in architecture that determined the functional character of buildings constructed in the 1960s for FSU's Science Center.

Nursing Building

Location: east of Leach Student Recreation Center

The square mass of the red-brick building with bands of recessed windows and balconies occupied by the Florida State School of Nursing complements the other modern buildings in the FSU Science Center. The four-story structure was built to accommodate the teaching programs of the school, which was established in 1950. It contains classrooms and lecture halls, faculty offices, and laboratories. On the third floor, the Learning Resource Center provides undergraduate and graduate students with convenient access to books and publications, computers, online search facilities, and audiovisual materials geared to the nursing curriculum.

Nursing Building

FAMU/FSU School of Engineering

Location: 2525 Pottsdamer Street, across from the Seminole Golf Course, two miles southwest of the main campus.

L ocated adjacent to Innovation Park and west of the main campuses of the two universities that share its space and mission, this gleaming three-story complex of offices, classrooms, and laboratories is the result of a joint endeavor to educate undergraduate and graduate students in a range of engineering specialties: chemical, civil, electrical, industrial, and mechanical. The custom-designed building with strip windows, smooth metal-paneled surfaces, porthole windows, open spaces, and a cool, silvery-blue-and-gray color scheme provides a futuristic ambiance, enhanced by the eye-catching abstract sculptures suspended in the spacious atrium and arcade. The College of Engineering opened in

FAMU/FSU School of Engineering

1982 with fewer than fifty students: the enrollment is now more than two thousand. Its status as a joint college serving two universities builds on the heritage of FAMU as an educational institution for African Americans and that of FSU as a college for women, in that it emphasizes the diversity of its student and faculty population and the need to bring minorities and women into the future of engineering. Faculty and students work on practical and theoretical problems in areas such as robotics, structural analysis of bridges, aeroacoustics, the tidal flow of coastal rivers, and computer processes.

FAMU/FSU School of Engineering

Mendenhall Maintenance Complex

Location: Woodward Avenue

Colonel Herbert D. Mendenhall, for whom the FSU maintenance complex was named, was the resident engineer for FSCW/FSU from 1930 until 1953. In addition to supervising the campus buildings and grounds, he developed the master plan for the western half of the campus, which expanded so rapidly in the 1950s and 1960s when FSU became a coeducational univer-

Mendenhall Maintenance Complex

sity and science research center. Mendenhall was a cofounder of the Florida Engineering Society and was the organization's president from 1926 to 1927. The Mendenhall Building, the hub of campus planning and facilities, contains offices, shops, and storage areas.

Smith Hall

Location: Chieftain Way

The first residence hall built for men was originally called West Hall. Built in 1952 and considered in its architectural distinction to be "masculine and attractive," the eleven-story building had a ballroom on the first floor and a sundeck on the roof, but no air-conditioning. The largest residence hall on campus, it was home to more than 550 young men: air-conditioning was added and it became a coed dorm in the early 1970s. The contemporary boxlike shape of the light-colored brick building is softened by the curvilinear wall joining the two wings, a vertical row of porthole windows, and the flaring shape of the entrance. Smith Hall honors mathematics and physics Professor Elmer Riggs Smith, who served on the faculty of FSCW from

Smith Hall

1905 to 1942. He was one of President Albert A. Murphree's first faculty choices for Florida Female College, as FSU was called when it became the state-supported women's college. The 560 students who reside in Smith Hall at the end of the century still find some built-in furniture in their double rooms, as the first occupants did, but the rooms are now wired for computers and cable TV.

Kellum Hall

Location: Palmetto Drive

K ellum Hall, completed in 1959, was the second men's residence hall built on the main campus after FSCW became FSU and enrolled a growing number of male students. The

Kellum Hall

eleven-story modern skyscraper stood out boldly west of the older buildings, signaling more future growth in that direction. The dormitory housed more than 550 men, who enjoyed many modern amenities as well as a fabulous view. It has been a coed dorm since 1972, but the residents still find built-in furniture in their double rooms, just as the first students did. Kellum Hall was named for John Gabriel Kellum, FSCW's astute business manager from 1907 to 1945. In addition to establishing the college farm to provide a reliable source of fresh food for the dining hall, he was responsible for all manner of other practical matters such as setting up a bakery, laundry, bookstore, bank, and post office on campus. He can also be thanked for improving the landscaping and beautifying the grounds, as well as for his shrewd real-estate purchases that added hundreds of acres of valuable land to the mere 13.5 acres that made up the original campus.

Rogers Hall

Location: Palmetto Drive

This modern residence hall was named for Dr. William Hudson Rogers, professor emeritus of English from 1922 to 1964. Very well liked by the students, Dr. Rogers was named FSU's first Distinguished Professor in 1957. He served as chair of the English department from 1947 to 1956 and was an authority on the English poet Robert Browning. His interpretive readings of the works of Browning and Shakespeare were particularly popular with his students. Like most of the buildings constructed on the FSU campus in the 1950s and 1960s, Rogers Hall was influenced by new building technology and the International Style with its flat roof, strong vertical and horizontal lines, smooth surfaces, and greater mass and volume. The red-brick curtain walls on the main facade are blocked into rectangles, creating a bold geometric design. The eight-story apartment building, completed and dedicated in 1965, was home to almost two hundred men. Today the coed residence hall accommodates single graduate students in apartments, each equipped with a kitchen.

Rogers Hall

McCollum Hall

Location: Palmetto Drive

This ten-story skyscraper residence hall was named for Miss Edith McCollum, director of housing from 1941 to 1970. During her time, six new dormitories were added and the student population grew from 1,434 to 4,268. A native of Mayo, Florida, she received her bachelor's degree from FSCW in 1927 and taught in public schools before taking her administrative position at FSCW. McCollum Hall, which opened in 1975, was designed for apartment living rather than having more traditional dorm rooms. It is now the home of 238 men and women above the

McCollum Hall

first-year level who share townhouse and efficiency apartments. The deeply recessed windows and balconies and the strong vertical lines of the dormitory reflect modern design trends, and the building's cast-concrete facade was a departure from the tradition of brick exterior walls that provides a strong visual unity to the campus.

Salley Hall

Location: Call Street

The twin towers of Salley Hall marked a new era in student housing when they opened in 1964. This was the first coed dorm on the FSU campus: men occupied one tower and women resided in the other, but they shared the recreation area that connects the tower blocks. Influenced by the International Style with its flat roof, smooth walls, and a structural skeleton covered by a thin nonstructural outer skin, Salley proved to be a winner with student residents. Instead of dorm rooms, living space was organized into apartments or suites. Today 574 students fill the two towers. The residence hall honors Dr. Nathaniel Moss Salley, first dean of the School of Education, who served in that capacity from 1915 to 1937. He spent thirty-five years of his long career as a professional educator at FSCW and retired in 1945.

Salley Hall

Stone Building and FSU School

Location: Call Street

The tradition of preparing teachers for Florida public schools began on this campus in 1901, when twenty-four students enrolled for the Normal Course, or teacher training. Since then, thousands of Florida teachers have received their "basic training" here. The FSCW School of Education formerly occupied the Psychology Building next to Westcott, but by the 1970s this rapidly growing division of FSU was so pressed for space that its offices and classrooms were spread over more than twenty different buildings on campus. At one time, classes were held in the old World War II military buildings at the old Dale Mabry Field. The College of Education is now housed in the

Stone Building

Mode L. Stone Building, a four-story brick building with deeply recessed windows, completed in 1978 on the west side of the campus. The Stone Building honors Dr. Mode L. Stone, a native Floridian who became dean in 1956, a position he held until his retirement in 1973. South of the Stone Building is the Florida State University School, built between 1953 and 1954. Affiliated with the College of Education, this K-12 school, which draws its students from all over the Tallahassee area, serves as a developmental research school and practice teaching facility.

Tully Gym

Location: Chieftain Way

In 1956, the Tully Gym replaced the old military-built gym on West Campus, a former World War II pilot training base, as the home of the Seminoles basketball team. It was not air-conditioned until 1975, making it the "hottest place in town" for

Tully Gym

hoop fans. When bad weather rained out Doak Campbell Stadium, graduation ceremonies were held in the gym. Both basketball games and graduation exercises are now held at the Tallahassee–Leon County Civic Center, but the Tully Gym is still used for practice by the men's and women's varsity basketball teams. It is the home of the Lady Seminoles volleyball team as well as of the FSU physical education department. New bleachers were installed in 1993, with seating for more than two thousand fans. The state-of-the-art weight room in the Tully Gym is used for fitness training by all Lady Seminoles student-athletes. The facility honors Robert Henry (Bobby) Tully. A football letterman, the popular Seminoles athlete graduated in 1952 and died two years later after a long illness.

Leach Student Recreation Center

Location: Chieftain Way

Leach Student Recreation Center

F lorida State students keep fit and trim in the recreation complex completed in 1991. It was named for Dr. Bobby E. Leach, vice president for student affairs and the first African American to be appointed to the position of vice president at FSU. A sixteen-lane pool with four diving boards is used by the men's and women's swimming and diving teams and is also available to other students at specified times. Fitness machines, a variety of courts and exercise areas, a jogging course, and an aerobics room help students stay in condition, build strength, and relieve stress. Other amenities for relaxation and socialization are the attractive atrium lounge, the sauna and hot tubs, and the health bar. The cantilevered, curving upper story accented by a bold stripe of windows on the west facade creates a dynamic architectural contrast to the red-brick base of the building.

Other Athletic Facilities

Locations: Various

F SU continually upgrades and improves its athletic and sports recreation facilities. As a member of the Atlantic Coast Conference, FSU fields seventeen varsity intercollegiate teams.

Seminoles swimmers and divers use the pool in the Leach Student Recreation Center as well as the one in the Stults Aquatic Center near the Oglesby Student Union. This inviting outdoor complex was named for N. Bauman "Bim" Stults, head coach of the FSU swimming and diving teams for twenty-five years.

Tennis buffs watch the Seminoles varsity court stars practice and compete at the award-winning Scott Speicher Tennis Center, which can accommodate one thousand fans. The center, which was named for Lieutenant Commander Michael Scott Speicher, an FSU graduate and the first American casualty during Operation Desert Storm, is a major enhancement for the Donald Loucks Courts.

Stults Aquatic Center (top) and Scott Speicher Tennis Center (bottom)

Loucks, for whom the twelve courts were named, came to FSCW in 1936 as a professor of physical education. In 1947 he became FSU's first men's basketball coach and coach of the tennis team.

The new Lady Seminoles stadium facility for the women's soccer and softball teams pays respect to the collegiate-Gothic architectural traditions of the UF campus with gable roofs, red brick, and stone trim. The complex features a baseball diamond on the east side and the soccer field on the west side.

The Dick Howser Stadium, one of the finest college baseball stadiums in the country, draws enthusiastic crowds of university and hometown boosters to its games. The covered stadium and bleachers can seat five thousand fans. Dick Howser, for whom the facility was named, was FSU's first baseball all-American and later played professionally for the Kansas City Royals.

The Mike Long Track was named for FSU's first track-and-field coach; he built the Seminoles track-and-field team into one of the best in the nation during his twenty-three-year career. A strength and training facility and coaches' offices are located in the field house, and the stadium can seat fifteen hundred fans for outdoor meets.

The nineteen-hole Seminole Golf Course is located two miles west of the university, adjacent to Innovation Park and the FAMU/FSU School of Engineering.

Haskins Circus Complex

Location: Chieftain Way

FSU's Flying High Circus is the only all-student college circus in the nation. It was established in 1947 by Jack Haskins, a professor of physical education who developed and directed

Haskins Circus Complex

the circus program until his retirement in 1964. Although Haskins never performed in a circus himself, some of his stars have received offers from professional circus companies. Students not only perform on the flying trapeze, swinging trapeze, and Spanish web, and as jugglers and clowns, but also set up and rig all the equipment. The Flying High Circus, which is self-supporting, has appeared on television and has state, national, and international performances to its credit. Each spring the circus troupe treats Tallahassee to a spectacular show. In 1986 the practice lot, where the bright Garnet and Gold tent can often be seen, was dedicated to Jack Haskins, who was elected to the FSU Hall of Fame in 1979.

Doak Campbell Stadium and University Center

Location: Stadium Drive and Pensacola Street

The home of FSU Seminoles football began as a playing field in a former pasture with bleacher seating for fifteen thousand fans. It was built in 1950, three years after the coeducational university was established. Football became an important part of campus life, and through the years the team and its outstanding record became legendary. The stadium, enlarged many times, was named for Doak S. Campbell, who led the school through its transition from FSCW to FSU, serving as president from 1941 to 1957. In the early 1990s, approximately four hundred thousand square feet of extra space for offices, classrooms, and service facilities were created by wrapping the seven-story University Center around Doak Campbell Stadium. The enhanced structure makes a strong architectural statement by relating to the Gothic

Doak Campbell Stadium

University Center

style used on the original buildings. With gables, towers, arches, and arcades, and the use of red brick and stone trim, the multi-use, horseshoe-shaped facility helps solve a chronic space problem and adds visual excitement to the west zone of the campus. It encompasses a book store, a food court, the elegant dining rooms of the University Center Club, academic and administrative offices, student services offices once scattered all over the campus, as well as FSU's School of Motion Picture, Television, and Recording Arts and its state-of-the-art studio facilities. The adjacent Coyle Moore Athletic Center and stadium seating were also expanded, and more parking spaces were created in anticipation of the increase in 'Noles fans eager to "be there" for the future football triumphs of the FSU Seminoles.

Heritage Tower

Location: Pensacola Street, north of Doak Campbell Stadium

The tower fountain given by the graduating classes of 1946–1948, the transitional classes during the time Florida State College for Women became Florida State University, continues the tradition of class gifts that was well established at

Heritage Tower

FSCW and marks the fiftieth anniversary of FSU. Like the fountain in front of the Westcott Building, given by the classes of 1915 and 1917, and the entrance gates, a gift of the classes of 1916 and 1918, this fiftieth-class-reunion project reflects the powerful bonds between the school's alumi and their alma mater. Sealed inside are materials that document the history and traditions of Florida State. The placement of the handsome commemorative tower at the west entrance to the university brings increased focus and distinction to this part of the campus. The three gleaming torches that crown the tower were chosen as a symbol of the institution in 1909. The Latin inscription identifies them as "Vires, Artes, Mores," representing the physical, mental, and moral ideal and purpose of higher education.

Suggested Reading

For more information about Tallahassee and Florida State University, you may wish to consult the following sources:

Chiles, Rhea, ed. *700 North Adams Street*. Tallahassee: Florida Governor's Mansion Foundation, 1997.

Conradi, Edward. *Memoirs of Edward Conradi*. Undated booklet in Special Collections of Strozier Library, Florida State University, Tallahassee.

Dunn, Hampton. *Yesterday's Tallahassee*. Miami: E. A. Beemann Publishing Co., 1974.

Ellis, Mary Louise, and William Warren Rogers. *Tallahassee and Leon County: A History and Bibliography*. Tallahassee: Florida Department of State, 1986.

Groene, Bertram A. *Ante-bellum Tallahassee*. Tallahassee: Florida Heritage Foundation, 1971.

Historic Tallahassee Preservation Board. *Capitol: A Guide for Visitors*. Tallahassee: Historic Preservation Board, 1982.

Sellers, Robin Jeanne. *Femina Perfecta: The Genesis of Florida State University*. Tallahassee: FSCW/FSU Class of 1947, 1995.

Wills, Martee, and Joan Perry Morris. *Seminole History: A Pictorial History of Florida State University*. Jacksonville: South Star Publishing Co., 1987.

Index

*Note: Page numbers in **bold** represent photos.*